GARY MITCHELL

Gary Mitchell was born in Rathcoole, North Belfast. In 1990 he wrote his first radio play, which won a BBC Radio 4 Young Playwright's Festival Award, and in 1995 became the first Protestant and first person from Northern Ireland to win the Stewart Parker Award for his play *Independent Voice*. In 1998, *In a Little World of Our Own* won the Irish Times Theatre Award for best new play and was performed for the Abbey Theatre's first ever visit to the Lyric, Belfast. In the same year, he was awarded the Belfast Drama Award for *In a Little World of Our Own* and *Sinking*. He was appointed Writer in Residence at the Royal National Theatre, London, in 1998, and his subsequent play, *Trust*, won the Pearson Best New Play prize. *The Force of Change* (Royal Court Theatre, 2000) won both the George Devine Award and the Evening Standard Charles Wintour Award for Most Promising Playwright. A television series based on *The Force of Change* is currently in development, and he is currently working on a new play, *Remorse*, at the Abbey Theatre, Dublin. The film of *As the Beast Sleeps* was screened at the 2001 Edinburgh Film Festival.

Other Titles in this Series

Gary Mitchell

AS THE
BEAST SLEEPS

NICK HERN BOOKS
London
www.nickhernbooks.co.uk

A Nick Hern Book

As The Beast Sleeps first published in Great Britain in 2001
as a paperback original by Nick Hern Books Limited,
14 Larden Road, London W3 7ST

As the Beast Sleeps copyright © 2001 Gary Mitchell

Gary Mitchell has asserted his right to be identified as
the author of this work

Cover design: 19/20

Typeset by Country Setting, Kingsdown, Kent CT14 8ES
Printed by LSL Press, Bedford, MK41 0TX

ISBN 1 85459 6519

A CIP catalogue record for this book is available
from the British Library

For my brother
Stephen
and my sister
Gail
and in memory of
Joe Ramone

As the Beast Sleeps received its London premiere in September 2001 at the Tricycle Theatre, directed by John Sheehan, with the following cast:

KYLE	Robert Donovan
SANDRA	Abigail McGibbon
FREDDIE	Michael Liebmann
LARRY	Simon Wolfe
JACK	Mark McCrory
NORMAN	Dessie Gallagher
ALEC	Derek Halligan

The same cast had previously performed *As the Beast Sleeps* at the Lyric Theatre, Belfast in May 2001, but for the following exceptions

LARRY	Colum Convey
NORMAN	Sean Kearns
ALEC	John Hewitt

The play's original premiere took place at the Peacock Theatre, Dublin in June 1998, directed by Conall Morrison, with the following cast:

KYLE	Stuart Graham
SANDRA	Cathy White
FREDDIE	Patrick O'Kane
LARRY	Colum Convey
JACK	Frank McCusker
NORMAN	Vincent Higgins
ALEC	Wesley Murphy

Characters

KYLE

SANDRA

FREDDIE

LARRY

JACK

NORMAN

ALEC

Scene One

Living room. Day.

KYLE *and* SANDRA (*she is not yet present*) *are in the process of decorating their house.* FREDDIE *and* KYLE *are scraping wallpaper from a wall each in the living room. Two basins of water, two cloths and two black plastic bags sit between them. One plastic bag is full of scraped wallpaper and tied, the other is nearly full.*

KYLE. I'm knackered. Do you want to stop and do the bag thing again?

FREDDIE. It's your house, mate.

KYLE *gets the black bag that is nearly full.* FREDDIE *piles more scrapings from the floor into it as* KYLE *holds it open. When they decide it is full enough* KYLE *ties it tight and throws it into the corner.*

KYLE. Cup of tea?

KYLE *sits in his chair indicating* FREDDIE *has to make the tea.*

FREDDIE. It's your turn.

KYLE. Fuck it. I'll wait.

FREDDIE *sits on the settee. They rest.* SANDRA *enters through the front door and makes her way into the living room. She is carrying bags of wallpaper.* FREDDIE *jumps up immediately, but she's in before he can get close enough to the wall.*

SANDRA. Have you's done anything?

KYLE. Unbelievable. Like fucking radar.

FREDDIE. Just sat down this second.

SANDRA. You say that every time.

FREDDIE. But this time it's true.

SANDRA. And what about all the other times then? Were they not true?

FREDDIE *starts scraping the walls again.*

KYLE. Make a wee cup of tea, Sandra.

SANDRA *sets the bag of wallpaper down and starts to take rolls from it and place them on the floor.*

SANDRA. What would you like with it – sandwiches or biscuits?

FREDDIE. I'd love a wee sandwich, I'm starving.

SANDRA. Cheese or ham?

FREDDIE. Cheese.

SANDRA. Where's the mop?

FREDDIE. What?

SANDRA. The mop. I want to tie it to my arse so as I can clean the kitchen floor while I'm feeding you's two.

KYLE. You're not funny. Go on and do it, we're knackered here.

SANDRA. And what am I?

FREDDIE. It's his turn. (*Smiles at* KYLE.) Just thought I'd mention that.

SANDRA. Is that what you's have been doing, sitting drinking tea all day?

KYLE. Look at the walls, Sandra. That's what we've been doing all day.

SANDRA *sets a couple of rolls of wallpaper beside her as she sits on the settee. She barely has time to sigh when she notices a scrap of wallpaper lying on the arm of the settee. KYLE notices her pick it up, so he gets up to go back to work.*

SANDRA. Sheets!

FREDDIE *avoids being told off by lifting his basin of water and going into the kitchen.*

SANDRA. I told you to cover these with sheets before you started.

KYLE. Couldn't find any.

SANDRA. Where did you look?

KYLE. Everywhere.

SANDRA. Did you look in the cupboard in the bedroom?

KYLE *dips the cloth in the basin and spreads the water onto the wallpaper.*

The cupboard we keep the old sheets in. You might have found them there.

FREDDIE *returns with his basin half full and a bottle of washing up liquid.*

FREDDIE. I just filled this and put the kettle on, I'm not making tea or anything. (*To* KYLE.) Do you want some of this?

SANDRA. What are you using that for?

KYLE. We're mixing it into the water.

SANDRA. Well I knew you weren't going to be putting it in the sink and doing any dishes with it. The question is – why are you putting it in the water?

KYLE. It helps you get the paper off.

SANDRA. That's an aul' wives tale.

FREDDIE. It works. As long as you let it soak in properly first but.

SANDRA. Good. That'll give you time to make me a cup of tea.

KYLE. Unbelievable.

SANDRA *has opened a roll of Rangers Football Club Wallpaper.*

SANDRA. What do you think of this?

KYLE. Where's it for?

SANDRA (*sarcastically*). In here.

KYLE. Do me.

FREDDIE. Fucking excellent.

SANDRA (*seriously*). It's for Joe's room, obviously.

KYLE. It could've been for the spare room.

SANDRA (*pretending to be serious*). I got us a lovely pink paper for the spare room.

KYLE. Pink?

SANDRA (*laughs*). Look at his face.

KYLE. We don't need any paper for the spare room.

SANDRA. Why, are we just going to leave it bare?

KYLE. For the time being.

SANDRA. Don't be stupid.

KYLE. If we've enough paint left over we'll just give the walls a quick coat.

FREDDIE. I don't think there'll be any paint left over.

SANDRA. It doesn't matter, we're not painting it.

KYLE. I'm not talking about painting it permanently Sandra. Temporary, just until we get a few quid and then you can have it whatever way you want.

SANDRA. I'll have it whatever way I want now.

KYLE. And how are you going to pay for it?

SANDRA. Same way as I paid for this lot. I'll get it off my Ma.

   KYLE *shakes his head and sighs.*

KYLE. You can't keep on borrowing money from your Ma. It has to be paid back.

SANDRA. So, we'll do that when we get a few quid.

KYLE. And until then we just have to listen to her moaning about it.

SANDRA. Don't you fucking start about my Ma – what did your Ma ever give us?

KYLE. You can't give what you haven't got.

SANDRA. She's plenty tucked away.

KYLE. And anyway, your Ma's never given us anything.

SANDRA. Where did all this come from then?

KYLE. Lendsies – there's a big difference.

FREDDIE. That reminds me, Sandra, your Ma asked me to keep a wee eye out for those Rangers quilts.

KYLE. What Rangers quilts?

SANDRA. I promised Joe I'd get them for his bed and my Ma said she'd go halfers. – and that's not lendsies. (*To* FREDDIE.) Any luck?

FREDDIE. I spoke to some boys who do that sort of caper and they're selling them for a couple of quid. So tell her if she wants me to get him one, I will.

KYLE. They're stolen.

FREDDIE (*sarcastically*). Seriously?

SANDRA. Get us the home one from me and the away one from my Ma.

KYLE. Don't bother. I'm getting him one for his birthday. A proper one.

FREDDIE. These are proper ones.

KYLE. They're not.

SANDRA. They are.

KYLE. They might be the same but to me it's the principle of the thing.

FREDDIE. And what would that be, you'd rather get ripped off by the shop owners than boys who are in the same boat as us? Because that's all it comes down to.

KYLE. No it's not, Freddie. If you buy anything out of the Official Rangers Club Shops it's guaranteed your money will be used to strengthen the squad, buy stolen shit off stealing bastards and the money goes down the fucking tubes.

FREDDIE. And you believe that?

KYLE. Yeah I do.

SANDRA. Well I don't care about strengthening the squad, all I care about is getting wee Joe off my back, he's been at me now about getting them for ages. (*Acts Joe.*) You promised.

KYLE. His birthday'll be soon enough.

SANDRA. No it won't, you don't have to tuck him in every night and hear him moaning about all the other wee fellas who have them already.

KYLE. See what you started here.

FREDDIE. I was only trying to do you's a favour.

Pause.

KYLE. I know you were and I appreciate it, but . . . It's the principle.

SANDRA. And what about the principle of having no money?

KYLE. I'll get us money.

SANDRA. When?

KYLE. As soon as I can.

FREDDIE. Maybe now's the time for another wee job, Kyle.

KYLE. There's still no jobs to be done, Freddie.

FREDDIE. That's because of all this shite that's going on. We need to do something about that, Kyle. Maybe start doing things on our own.

KYLE. That's the last thing we need to do.

SANDRA. Maybe Freddie's right.

KYLE. Don't be stupid, Sandra.

SANDRA. Don't you 'Don't be stupid' me.

FREDDIE. I'm just saying – think about it.

KYLE. Do you think I haven't thought about it?

FREDDIE. Have you?

KYLE. Of course I've thought about it. But trust me here – both of you – all we have to do is bide our time.

SANDRA. You've been saying that for ages now.

KYLE. I know.

FREDDIE. And things are just getting worse. When did you ever hear of any of us being barred from the club? It's our fucking club for fuck's sake. How can you get barred from your own club?

KYLE. I'm going to talk to someone about that.

FREDDIE. Who?

KYLE. Larry.

FREDDIE. I've heard he doesn't cut it any more.

KYLE. Don't be stupid.

SANDRA (*mocking* KYLE). Don't be stupid. Don't be stupid. (*As herself.*) Do you ever think for just one second that maybe it's you who's being stupid?

KYLE (*more determined*). I've said I'm going to talk to someone about it. Now, get off my fucking back about it.

They do. KYLE *watches* FREDDIE *work as* SANDRA *sits quietly, simmering.*

Look, Dougie and Mac fucked up, all right. And so did you Freddie, you're lucky you're not barred as well.

FREDDIE. Somebody had to do something – them dickheads are getting out of hand. Fucking Jack thinks he fucking runs the place now.

KYLE. He does, Freddie.

FREDDIE. I know he fucking, runs it – runs it, but you know what I mean . . . Fuck him!

SANDRA. When are you going to speak to Larry?

KYLE. As soon as I see him. (*Pause.*) He's a busy man, he's a lot on his plate at the moment.

SANDRA. Unlike us. So when you do see him you may ask him to put his hand in his pocket.

KYLE. I will.

FREDDIE. And get the boys back into the club.

KYLE. Don't worry about that either.

SANDRA. OK. Tea – who's turn is it?

FREDDIE. His.

KYLE. We'll get tea in a minute. Just show me what you got for in here?

SANDRA *takes another roll and starts to roll it out to view.*

SANDRA. This is for in here.

KYLE. Dead on.

SANDRA *searches in the bag.*

SANDRA. I was thinking of a wee border between that and the top bit would be just plain white.

KYLE *sits again.*

FREDDIE. Hey! Am I doing this by myself now.

KYLE. Sandra, you do the tea and we'll finish this off.

SANDRA. No, it's your turn.

KYLE. It's always my turn.

SANDRA. Well, when are you going to do it? And then it won't be no more.

KYLE *stands, resigned.*

KYLE. Oh, all right.

KYLE *makes his way to the kitchen.* FREDDIE *continues to scrape his wall and* SANDRA *rolls the wallpaper back up and places it beside the other rolls.*

Scene Two

Punishment Room. Evening.

The room is almost completely empty. Four small, wooden chairs are lined across one wall. An old, worn out table takes centre stage. LARRY sits in front of it, reflecting. ALEC enters the room. ALEC is wearing a suit and LARRY is more casually dressed.

ALEC. They told me I'd find you here. What's going on?

LARRY. I haven't been in this room in years.

ALEC. That's good, isn't it?

LARRY. This is where it all began for me.

ALEC. Yeah, but in what seat?

LARRY (*smiles*). It's changed a bit. The young fellas have
their own methods now. The first time – I was sitting in that
corner, watching. There was more seats than this. Our
Richie was running the show then.

ALEC. Where did he sit?

LARRY *begins to arrange the room and continues as he
speaks.*

LARRY. This seat would have been for the offender, right?
(*Places one seat where he reckons the middle of the room is,
facing forward.*) Richie would have sat in one of these ones.
(*Drags two seats across the floor and lines them directly
behind the offender's.*) See they sat behind him, out of sight,
know what I mean? (*Gets the other seat and places it in the
line.*) Richie always said that the real damage was done in
their imagination. Nothing we could show them or threaten
them with could hurt them as much as just sitting behind
them, doing nothing. They would do it to themselves.

ALEC. But some of them must have needed a bit more than
imagination.

LARRY. Oh yeah, but it was always a good start. Never stand
in front of him. Never let him see exactly what you're
doing. But every now and again, a flash. Something to start
them thinking. They won't know exactly what they seen. A
knife, gun. Garden clippers, a spade. A saw. Who knows
what their fear would throw at them?

ALEC. A bit like Hitchcock.

LARRY (*considers for a moment*). Our Richie could scare a
man so much without actually doing anything, it was . . .
frightening, even just to know. I don't know how to explain
it to you, Alec.

ALEC. I've heard the stories.

LARRY. Maybe that was the key – the stories. Everybody knew a Richie story, or at least that's the way it seemed when I was a kid.

ALEC. Well, why don't we forget about stories? Jack said you wanted to see me. (*Pause.*) Is there a problem with the club?

LARRY. No, the club's fine.

ALEC. Money?

LARRY. You'll get your money. (*Quickly.*) We've another big fat donation to the new cause.

ALEC. It's the same cause, Larry. Just a different way of fighting for it. Is that what the problem is?

LARRY. No.

ALEC. I thought you understood all that, Larry.

LARRY. I do. That's what I want to talk to you about.

ALEC. Then talk to me.

LARRY *thinks.*

LARRY. This room . . .

ALEC. Forget about this room, Larry. We've taken great steps to move people away from rooms like this.

LARRY. See when you talk like that, you still sound like you're on TV.

ALEC. If we get things right, rooms like this will disappear from Ulster forever.

LARRY. You're doing it again, Alec.

ALEC *stops.*

LARRY. Do you know what the worst part of this room is?

ALEC. I don't think there is a worst part.

LARRY. But one thing always bothered me – and still does.

ALEC. Somebody die?

LARRY. No, nothing like that.

ALEC. What then?

LARRY. There was only ever three Catholics in this room.

ALEC. Did they get killed?

LARRY. One nearly did. He was given to us, by the Police. They wanted a confession. We scared the shite out of him, they came in and rescued him, and he confessed all right. Probably would've confessed to anything they would have asked him to.

ALEC. That's terrible.

LARRY. That's the way it is.

ALEC. Was.

Silence.

LARRY. Do you remember Hughie? Would you know him? He went into politics like you. I think he was into the peace people and all that.

ALEC. What about him?

LARRY. He married a Catholic.

ALEC. And you brought her here?

LARRY. He did. (*Pause.*) Do you know what for?

ALEC. What?

LARRY. Sex. Right on this table. So he says. Some kind of fantasy thing.

ALEC. He's sick.

LARRY. He's a politician.

ALEC. Who was number three?

LARRY. Number three was one of us.

ALEC. A Catholic?

LARRY. Well, his Ma was. I suppose she tried to make him one, but it didn't work. Wrong location.

ALEC. And what was he doing here?

LARRY. He wanted to be here. He loved this stuff. Funny thing is, he jacked it in for the same reason as me.

ALEC. Which was?

LARRY. All our victims were Protestants.

ALEC. Yeah, but they were bad guys, right?

LARRY. What makes a man a bad guy? A black hat or a scar on his face? It's not that easy.

ALEC. Nobody said it was easy.

LARRY. It's funny, when I think of the old days, I remember them a bit like that. It all seems to have been easier then. And I even think of them in black and white. The Prods were the good guys and the taigs were the baddies. Simple as that.

ALEC. Well! Thanks for the trip down memory lane. But let me tell you this, Larry. I have always seen the world in blinding Technicolor. And I've seen too many bad Prods. Our own leaders, I couldn't support them. I just never felt like they represented me – or us. It was as though they lived in a different world and when you look at their lifestyle, let me tell you, you wouldn't be too far wrong. They're either very rich or very Christian, I don't know, but what I do know is this, being a Unionist or being a Protestant doesn't guarantee you being a nice person – same as your deal with the hat and the scar. (*Pause.*) Shall we go?

ALEC *walks to the door.*

LARRY. I want to hang around here a while.

Silence.

ALEC. Is there something else you want to talk to me about, Larry?

LARRY. There is.

ALEC. Well, let's go somewhere else and you can tell me why I had to miss a very important meeting to come all the way over here.

LARRY. I have a problem, Alec. Is that not important?

ALEC. Of course it is, that's why I'm here. Now let's sort it out.

LARRY. I don't know how we can do that.

ALEC. Talk to me.

LARRY. It's the young fellas.

ALEC. What about them?

LARRY. That's my problem.

ALEC. What ones are we talking about? Specifically.

LARRY. The young men that I have invested more than ten years of my life in.

ALEC. What about them?

LARRY. I don't know what to say to them.

ALEC. Everything's going to be all right. Tell them that.

LARRY. They're not all thick, you know – some of them will want everything explained.

ALEC *thinks.*

ALEC. What do you suggest?

LARRY. You tell me.

ALEC. They're your boys. You have to talk to them.

LARRY. I can't.

ALEC. Tell them not to worry and . . . Not to get excited. Everything's fixed.

LARRY *walks away from* ALEC.

LARRY. Forget about it.

ALEC. What? (*Pause.*) What?

LARRY. I know what has to be done, Alec. Talking is for us and for the future. Not for these boys. They don't talk, they don't listen. They follow orders. I made them that way.

ALEC. Well then order them to do what you want them to do.

LARRY. Don't you worry about it, big Larry'll fix it.

ALEC. In here?

LARRY. If I have to.

ALEC. Larry?

LARRY. I said forget about it. Just think about this. Afterwards, after I sort this lot out I want something sorted out for me.

ALEC. What like?

LARRY. I want in.

ALEC. In what exactly?

LARRY. In politics. In your team.

ALEC. Larry . . .

LARRY. What, you don't think I can do it?

ALEC. Let me think about it.

LARRY. If I can convince these young fellas to change their minds I can do anything.

ALEC. Yeah, but what you have to understand is you can't bring people into this room and make them vote for you – politics doesn't work like that.

LARRY. Well then you're going to have to teach me how it does work.

ALEC. We'll see.

LARRY. I mean it, Alec. I'm not going to be left behind.

ALEC. Of course you're not. But who would look after the club?

LARRY. Jack can do the lot if he's backed up properly.

ALEC *thinks.*

ALEC. There's a lot of money there, Larry. Can he be trusted?

LARRY. Of course he can.

ALEC. Let me talk to some people for you and see what they think. That's the best I can do for now.

LARRY. You have to promise me Alec, that even if they think it's a bad idea, you'll do everything that you can to change their minds for me.

ALEC. Of course I will.

LARRY. Because if you can't change their minds for me then maybe I can't change these young fellas' minds for you.

ALEC. Are you threatening me?

LARRY. Just promise me.

ALEC. Have I ever lied to you?

LARRY. Let me put it like this, you've never lied to me and I've never threatened you. Let's go.

LARRY *leaves the room.* ALEC *hesitates, looks around and then follows quickly after him.*

Scene Three

Bar. Night.

There is one small table with three chairs and a pool table, complete with wall-racks of pool cues, near the door at the back of the bar that leads to the offices. SANDRA *sits at the table, looking around. A pint glass sits on the other side of the table.* KYLE's *leather jacket is hanging over another chair.* SANDRA *searches the pockets as* KYLE *approaches with a pint of lager, a Bacardi and a tin of coke.*

KYLE. Help yourself.

SANDRA *finds a lighter, which she uses to light her cigarette.*

SANDRA. What are you doing hiding away round here?

KYLE. I'm watching the door.

SANDRA (*pouring a little coke into her Bacardi*). People get paid to do that. (*Points at pool table.*) Do you want another lesson?

KYLE. No, I've been playing since I got here.

SANDRA. It's all right for some.

FREDDIE *shouts from off stage.*

FREDDIE. Kyle?

KYLE *looks in that direction and smiles.*

KYLE. Freddie! (*To* SANDRA.) He'll give you a game.

FREDDIE *appears walking towards the table, he stops and holds his arms out.*

FREDDIE. Who wants first hug?

KYLE *stands.* SANDRA *watches, smiling as they hug.*

KYLE. What's happening?

FREDDIE *ignores the question and holds his arms out again.*

FREDDIE. Sandra!

SANDRA *lifts her glass in the air.*

SANDRA. Bacardi.

FREDDIE *spins round away from the table.*

FREDDIE. Jimmy!

KYLE. Jimmy's not on tonight.

FREDDIE *turns back towards the table.*

FREDDIE. Who's on?

KYLE. Paul and Sadie.

FREDDIE (*shouts*). Sadie.

NORMAN *approaches* FREDDIE.

NORMAN. Is there a problem?

FREDDIE. What like?

KYLE. No, no problem, Norman.

NORMAN. What's all the shouting about then?

FREDDIE. I'm trying to get a fucking drink, why?

KYLE. Sit down, Freddie.

NORMAN. Are you going to start again tonight?

KYLE. There's no problem I said, Norman.

NORMAN. If you want to order a drink go to the bar.

SANDRA. Who rattled your cage?

FREDDIE. What the fuck's waitresses for?

NORMAN. There's no waitresses on yet, so as I said, if you want a drink you'll have to go to the bar.

KYLE. You've made your point, Norman. Leave it at that.

NORMAN *turns and walks away.* KYLE *gets up.*

SANDRA. Where are you going?

FREDDIE. Do you see what I'm saying now, Kyle? Who started that?

KYLE. Sit down and relax, I'll get you a drink. (*To* SANDRA.) Watch that door for me, will you?

KYLE *walks off towards the bar.* FREDDIE *goes to the pool table.*

FREDDIE. Do you want a game?

SANDRA. What are we playing – fiver a go?

FREDDIE. I couldn't take your money off you now.

SANDRA. Don't worry, you won't get a chance.

FREDDIE. You can talk the talk but can you use the chalk?

SANDRA. You're going to need to get a word that rhymes with cue, Freddie.

SANDRA *sets the balls up then rolls the white gently towards the opposite end of the table before handing the black ball to* FREDDIE. FREDDIE *places the black in the triangle and steps aside.*

FREDDIE. Ladies first do your worst.

SANDRA (*lifts triangle off table and breaks*). Set your fiver down.

FREDDIE. I don't have a fiver.

SANDRA. Much have you?

FREDDIE. I've about one seventy.

SANDRA. Not for long.

KYLE *returns with no drinks.*

KYLE. Has anybody come out of Jack's office yet?

FREDDIE. No, why?

KYLE. Just wondering. (*To* SANDRA.) Have you any money on you?

SANDRA. Not much, but I'm about to get one seventy off Freddie here.

KYLE. Fuck it, it doesn't matter. I'll see you in a minute.

SANDRA. What do you need money for?

KYLE. Never mind, just stay here and watch that door.

KYLE goes back towards the bar area.

FREDDIE. What was that all about?

SANDRA. No idea.

FREDDIE. Will I go and see what the problem is?

SANDRA. No, your man Norman'll only start on you again.

FREDDIE. You've noticed that have you?

SANDRA. He's just a dickhead, don't let him annoy you.

FREDDIE. That's the thing but, he's allowed to annoy me, do you know what I mean? If I say anything back, I'm starting something.

SANDRA. I know all about it.

FREDDIE. Does Kyle but?

SANDRA. Of course he does and he's going to be doing something about him.

FREDDIE. When but?

SANDRA. Very soon.

FREDDIE. The sooner the better. They're doing my fucking head in. Especially now with Dougie and Mac not even being allowed in. Things are getting fucking out of hand, Sandra.

SANDRA. Not for much longer.

The game goes on.

FREDDIE. So, how's the wee lad?

SANDRA. Dead on. We had our dinner with my Ma. He's staying with her again tonight.

FREDDIE. He'll be thinking he lives there.

SANDRA. I know, but we couldn't have him in the house while all the painting's being done.

FREDDIE (*pretending to be serious*). Yeah but you have to watch yourself.

SANDRA. What do you mean?

FREDDIE. He'll get a complex about it.

SANDRA (*thinks* FREDDIE*'s joking*). Fuck off, Freddie.

FREDDIE. Seriously, that sort of thing can really fuck a kid's head up. Thinking his Ma's never there like. Probably think she doesn't love him and . . .

SANDRA. I'll fuck your head up in a minute.

FREDDIE *laughs.* SANDRA *misses a shot.*

SANDRA. I'm taking that again.

FREDDIE. No way.

SANDRA. I am, you put me off there.

SANDRA *prepares to take the shot again.*

FREDDIE. Fuck me.

SANDRA. What?

FREDDIE. That's not where it was.

SANDRA. Don't start. That is exactly where it was.

FREDDIE. All right, if you want to win by cheating, go ahead.

As SANDRA *goes to take her shot* FREDDIE *coughs and puts her off.* SANDRA *misses again and starts laughing.*

SANDRA. I'm taking that again too.

FREDDIE. Sure just keep hitting it, you're bound to pot it sooner or later.

SANDRA *prepares to take the shot again but can't because* FREDDIE *is distracting her. Finally, she stops laughing and focuses properly.*

(*Suddenly nudges* SANDRA *and speaks quickly.*) Where's he gone for this drink?

SANDRA. Stop fucking about Freddie.

FREDDIE. I'm only asking.

SANDRA. Sadie's probably giving him a bit of an ear bashing.

FREDDIE. Fuck I know. She's dynamite once she gets going.

SANDRA. You don't call her Machine gun Sadie for nothing.

FREDDIE. Is that why she's called that? (*Waits, smiling.*
SANDRA *doesn't laugh but takes a shot.* FREDDIE *thinks
of something else.*) Listen to this.

FREDDIE *winks at* SANDRA *and calls towards the bar.*

Sadie put that man down for fuck's sake.

SANDRA (*joins in*). You don't know where he's been.

FREDDIE. I do! And I can tell you if you knew . . .

SANDRA (*interrupts*). Hey!

FREDDIE. Fuck!

NORMAN *approaches again.*

SANDRA. Here we go again.

FREDDIE. Are you back?

NORMAN. There's other people in this bar trying to enjoy
themselves. Now I've already asked you to keep it down.

FREDDIE. Norman, let me explain something to you.

KYLE *returns with the drinks.*

KYLE. That was my fault big man. I took too long getting
these thirsty people their drinks.

NORMAN *steps away to let* KYLE *reach the table and
place the drinks down.* FREDDIE *watches* SANDRA.

NORMAN. That's all right, Kyle, but I've already been over
once.

KYLE. Sure, no problem. Don't worry about it.

FREDDIE. Worry about me kicking your arse all round this
bar.

KYLE*'s attention is taken away as the door to the office
opens and* JACK *steps in to the bar area.* SANDRA *laughs
at* NORMAN.

NORMAN. Are you threatening me?

FREDDIE. Do you want to make something of it?

KYLE. Go away, Norman.

KYLE *speaks as he gets up and begins to approach* JACK. JACK *comes to meet him half way.*

NORMAN. I'm just doing my job here.

JACK. What seems to be the problem?

KYLE. There's no problems, has Larry been here today?

NORMAN. These people are getting very loud. (*To* SANDRA.) No offence love.

SANDRA. I'm not your love.

NORMAN (*to* JACK). I was just asking them to keep it down.

JACK. Do I have to take steps here?

KYLE. I asked you a question, Jack.

JACK. You've asked me a thousand times, Kyle. And the answer is still the same. As soon as Larry gets here you will be the first to know. That's if you're still here.

KYLE. I will be.

JACK. Well, you can stay here as long as you respect the rules.

KYLE (*to* NORMAN). Go away and leave us alone. (*To everyone.*) We're just going to have a quiet drink and wait.

NORMAN. Make sure it's quiet.

KYLE *points at* NORMAN.

KYLE. Jack.

FREDDIE. What are you going to do if it's not? Two against two, what do you say, Kyle?

JACK *begins to back away, signalling towards the bar.*

SANDRA. Are you looking for help, Jack? (*As much to alert* KYLE.)

KYLE *watches* JACK.

JACK. In two seconds it can be ten against two.

FREDDIE. I like them odds.

JACK. If I have to get help, Kyle, you'll not be able to wait here.

KYLE. Let's just relax.

JACK. Ask your friend to sit down.

KYLE. Freddie?

SANDRA (*points at* NORMAN). Make him go away. And stay away.

KYLE. Jack?

JACK. Norman.

> JACK *nods* NORMAN *away from the table.* NORMAN *pauses for a moment before walking away.* JACK *waits for everyone to be seated and then walks towards the main bar area.* KYLE *stops him.*

KYLE. I've just been to the bar, Jack. What's that all about?

JACK. New place, new rules, Kyle. If you don't like them maybe you should consider drinking somewhere else.

KYLE. I'm fine here. Just you let me know when Larry arrives and we'll see what he thinks about your new rules.

> JACK *walks away.* FREDDIE *smiles and drinks.* SANDRA *finishes her drink.*

SANDRA. Who's going to go and get me another drink now?

> KYLE *sighs, his pint still almost full.*

KYLE. You're hitting it a bit heavy tonight, aren't you?

SANDRA. What are you talking about? I've had one drink with my dinner.

> FREDDIE *goes to get up but* KYLE *stops him.* FREDDIE *looks to* SANDRA. *They wait.*

I'll get it myself. (*To* FREDDIE.) Same again?

> FREDDIE *nods and drinks.*

KYLE. You'll have to pay for them.

SANDRA. What?

KYLE. New place, new rules.

FREDDIE. You're joking.

> FREDDIE *gets up.* KYLE *stops him again.*

KYLE. Where are you going?

FREDDIE. I'm going to go and see about that.

KYLE. There's no one to see.

FREDDIE. Sadie's there.

KYLE. Sadie's only doing her job, Freddie. Do you want to drop her in the shit or make her feel like a cunt? She could've let us order drinks all night and then asked us to pay up but she didn't. As soon as she seen me ordering again, she thought that was enough.

FREDDIE. Fuck that. Let's get fucking Jack back out here. And get him to explain how to fuck that works? I've risked my fucking life.

KYLE. We all have.

SANDRA. So, why don't you do something about it?

FREDDIE. Our team kept this place going for fuck sake. If it hadn't been for us robbing, they wouldn't have any beer to fucking sell. We'll not even mention all the other things that we've done.

KYLE. We haven't brought any beer here in ages.

FREDDIE. That's because they won't let us. I mean fuck me.

KYLE. Freddie, we didn't do what we did for free beer.

FREDDIE. I never said we did.

SANDRA. That's not what he means, Kyle.

KYLE. I know it's not what he means but that's what people will think he means if he tries to do something about it.

FREDDIE. Well, what are we going to do?

KYLE. We'll just wait, there's no point in talking with Jack, he's probably trying to make us do something to give him an excuse to bar us all. Larry has to be here sooner or later. When he arrives I'll talk to him – trust me the more things Jack does like this – the more reason Larry'll have to get rid of him.

FREDDIE. But I need a drink tonight and I've fuck all money.

SANDRA (*stands*). That's all right, I can pay.

SANDRA *checks in her pockets and comes up short. She stands still for a few seconds and then sits down.*

FREDDIE. What's the matter?

SANDRA. Haven't enough.

FREDDIE *quickly checks his pockets.*

FREDDIE. Thought you had a fiver for pool.

SANDRA. No, I was just going to take your money all night.

FREDDIE. That sorts that out.

SANDRA *stares at* KYLE. KYLE *watches the door to the offices.* FREDDIE *gets up and walks by the pool table.* KYLE *stands.* FREDDIE *takes a pool cue from the rack.*

KYLE. Give him another game, I'll get this round as well.

FREDDIE *unscrews the butt of the cue.*

FREDDIE. I'm not playing pool.

FREDDIE *passes* KYLE *on his way to the bar.* SANDRA *stands and watches* FREDDIE.

KYLE. Freddie? Fuck!

Scene Four

Private office. Day.

JACK *is sitting at his desk working on his computer.* NORMAN *enters from the main club area, his arm is in a sling.*

JACK. Come in and sit down.

NORMAN. Could we not do this like out in the bar over a few pints, Jack? You know, I look after you and you look after me.

JACK. Like you did last night?

NORMAN. That bastard came after me with a cue.

JACK. Well the good thing about it is that it strengthens our claim for tighter security.

NORMAN. Dead right.

JACK. I made a couple of calls first thing this morning. Larry will be coming in to look around and probably give the green light to a whole department. Which brings us back to this.

NORMAN. I'd still rather do all this caper over a wee drink.

JACK. Don't worry about it. Just relax.

JACK takes a print-out from his in-tray and begins to browse through it – waiting for NORMAN to relax.

NORMAN (*coming fully into the office, looking around it as he does so*). When are they going to finish in here?

JACK. They're doing the offices last. And after last night's damage that could be some time away.

NORMAN. Well, out there looks fantastic, did look fantastic . . .

JACK. And will look fantastic again.

NORMAN. You're doing a hell of a job, Jack. I mean that. I'm not trying to lick round you or anything. I really think you are.

JACK. Thanks Norman. Now listen to me, this isn't really an interview mate. The job's yours if you want it, all right?

NORMAN. Sure, sure. I understand. I want it like. But I have a few problems. Not with you.

JACK waits. NORMAN still looks around.

JACK. What kind of problems do you have, Norman?

NORMAN. It's Caroline. She told me that everything would be OK if it was over 200 quid a week.

JACK. It is over 200 quid a week – before tax. Do you understand that?

NORMAN. I heard it was 720.

JACK. A month, Norman. 720 quid a month is 180 quid a week in your hand, mate.

NORMAN. That's less than 200.

JACK. Yes it is, but Norman this is a real job, a permanent job. And that money will go up.

NORMAN. When?

JACK. Whenever.

NORMAN. Well she wants me to keep claiming the dole. Is that all right?

JACK. No, Norman. You won't be able to.

NORMAN. There's always ways, Jack.

JACK. Well that's between you and your wife, Norman, or your conscience, whatever. The thing is everything will be going through the books from now on and that means that you will be paying tax and a stamp and I've also arranged a pension scheme for you.

NORMAN. Pensioning me off already and I haven't even started work yet. That's lovely.

JACK. The lovely thing about it is, you don't have to worry about a thing. I'll be doing it all for you, so as all you'll have to do is your job.

NORMAN. Which is another thing I wanted to speak to you about.

JACK. What?

NORMAN. Do I have a uniform?

JACK. No. You just need to get yourself a good suit.

NORMAN. Will the other lads have uniforms?

JACK. There are no uniforms and there are no other lads.

NORMAN. Then how am I going to be Head of Security?

JACK. Officer in Charge of Security, Norman.

NORMAN. Oh, I thought there was going to be other people involved – like Jimmy and Paul and those guys. Shit! I told her I was going to be like a boss. I was trying to make it out like a sort of promotion, you know, she likes that sort of thing.

JACK. Eventually, you will be. But for the meantime they're just bar staff who, like last night, you will be able to call on if there's problems.

NORMAN. I'm not sure about that, Jack. I mean if Kyle hadn't have got hold of him . . . You know what I mean.

JACK. Well Kyle's not applying for any jobs and the nutcase won't be allowed back in, so . . .

NORMAN. Good.

Pause.

JACK. You see what everybody has to come to terms with, Norman is that this is a slow process. This will be a gradual thing. The money that's been borrowed for the refurbishment of this place will have to be paid back and that will hurt for a while but eventually we'll turn the corner and the money we make will be the money we're actually making for ourselves.

NORMAN. Well, can you talk to her for me? Tell her that.

JACK. All you have to tell her, Norman is what I'm telling you. From now on everything is above board, no more capering, no more nonsense. Do you understand? This is a good thing for you. And not just for you, but for your kids. And for Caroline. The pension, the insurance, all that is there to make sure her and the kids are all right no matter what happens.

NORMAN. What do you mean – no matter what happens?

JACK. You know, like if you had've been seriously hurt last night. Or if you had an accident.

NORMAN. What kind of accident?

JACK. Any kind of accident.

NORMAN. Something like a serious head injury, that sort of accident? Or if I got my arm completely ripped off like. Something like that?

JACK. That's what I'm trying to explain to you.

NORMAN. Fuck that! How could I get my arm ripped off?

JACK. You couldn't.

NORMAN. But you said there now that I could.

JACK. I'm talking about insurance.

NORMAN. Hold on a fucking minute, Jack.

JACK. What?

NORMAN. What kind of a fucking job have I got myself here?

JACK. Norman?

NORMAN. First I'm being pensioned off and now I'm having fucking accidents all over the place.

JACK. This is security I'm talking about.

NORMAN. Why can I not just do the doors like before? No accidents and no pensioning me off.

JACK. You're not listening to me, Norman.

NORMAN. I am listening to you.

JACK. If! Norman. If! Do you see, *if* you had an accident? Do you understand?

NORMAN (*thinks*). Well, listen Jack. You're going to have to explain it to her.

JACK. Norman she'll understand.

NORMAN. Would you not tell her for me? Like what if you brought Marie in for a drink or something and I brought her in and we just got together or something. She always likes doing things like that, you know what I mean?

JACK. Maybe dinner one night, what about that?

NORMAN. Where like?

JACK. Chimney Corner?

NORMAN. That's a bit expensive, but she'd love it like.

JACK. It'll be on me as a sort of welcome aboard dinner. Now I can't do any more than that, can I?

LARRY *enters the room and* JACK *signals to* NORMAN, *who greets him and takes his coat.*

NORMAN. Do you want me to go and get drinks, Jack?

JACK. Larry.

NORMAN. Do you want anything to drink, Larry?

LARRY (*points at* NORMAN's *arm*). Would you be able to carry anything?

NORMAN. Yes.

LARRY. Maybe later. First – business.

JACK. I've just appointed Norman, Officer in Charge of Security.

LARRY. Congratulations.

NORMAN. So will you have a wee drink to celebrate with me?

LARRY. When do you start?

NORMAN. I don't know.

JACK. You start now.

NORMAN. Excellent.

JACK. And that means – no drinks.

> KYLE *tries to make his way in.* NORMAN *attempts to stop his progress by closing the door on him.*

NORMAN. You can't come in here. This is a restricted area.

LARRY. Who is it?

NORMAN. Did you hear me? Stay out.

KYLE. I have to see Larry.

LARRY. Is there a problem?

KYLE. There is. Get away from the door.

NORMAN. Is he allowed in?

> KYLE *pushes in and grabs* NORMAN *by the sore arm.* NORMAN *yelps in pain as* KYLE *turns him against the wall and pushes his face up against it.*

KYLE. Do you want me to break this off for you?

JACK. Hey!

LARRY. Kyle? Can it wait two minutes?

KYLE. You won't piss off on me.

JACK. For God's sake.

LARRY. I only just got here. I'm not going anywhere.

KYLE. Sorry.

NORMAN. You will be.

KYLE. Don't ever get in my way again.

> NORMAN *is frozen to the spot, holding his sore arm.*
> KYLE *leaves the room.*

JACK. Are you all right, Norman?

NORMAN. I didn't want to hurt him, I was just trying to keep him out.

LARRY. Dangerous lad.

JACK. We'd need to get a lock on that door.

NORMAN. Is that part of my job?

JACK. Yes.

NORMAN. First thing tomorrow then.

LARRY. You better make it a big one.

JACK. That was one of the things I wanted to talk to you about, Larry. He's been waiting to see you here night after night. He just keeps asking if you're here and when we tell him that you're not he starts asking us when we think you're going to be here.

LARRY. Well, he knew I had to come here sooner or later.

NORMAN. What are we going to do about him? I could get Jimmy and Paul to throw him out if you want.

LARRY. Would three be enough?

NORMAN. I could throw him out myself if my arm was all right.

LARRY (*smiles*). What's the other problems, Jack?

JACK. Well, mostly the same.

LARRY. What like?

JACK. His mates. They've been doing a lot of slabbering. Making big claims, annoying people.

NORMAN. Getting everybody frightened.

JACK. Suspicious.

LARRY. Just them?

JACK. I don't know. I just think Kyle there has lost control of his team. You need to do something. Quick.

LARRY. Have you tried talking to them, Jack?

JACK. They won't listen to me.

NORMAN (*shows his arm*). They did this last night.

JACK. And you've seen the bar.

LARRY. I'll talk to him.

JACK. Good.

NORMAN. And if that doesn't work maybe me and some of the boys could talk to him. When I get off work I mean. Or is that part of my job as well?

JACK *shakes his head at* NORMAN.

JACK. No, Norman. But part of your job is to guard the door.

NORMAN *walks to the door and stops as though guarding it.*

From the outside.

NORMAN *leaves.*

LARRY. How's things going in the club?

JACK. Apart from them. I don't remember things being so good.

LARRY. Compared to last month?

JACK. Only slightly up, but last month was fantastic like, so this is an indication that things are going to level out in this way. Our own little peace dividend, you know.

LARRY. Our dividend comes later, Jack. First we have to take care of Alec.

JACK. That's something else I need to talk to you about.

LARRY. Fire away.

JACK. I won't bore you with the details. But I have to say this just. I think you're making a big mistake. I don't think you're giving us a fair chance here.

LARRY. What way do you mean?

JACK. The money we made last month should be used to pay off some of the debts. I've drawn up some proposals for you, I've got them on this disk. You can take that with you.

JACK takes a disk from the computer and passes it to LARRY.

LARRY. Disks are no good to me.

LARRY tosses the disk back onto the desk towards JACK.

Let me explain something to you, Jack. I don't care what your plans are for this place. I can look at it and it looks good. That's important, but what's more important is that I come in here every month and you give me a cheque for Alec. Do you understand what I'm saying to you?

JACK. But taking the money away at this stage could cripple us. We're doing well. But we could do better, Larry. If you just gave me a chance. In there I have a five year business plan.

LARRY. Five years is a long time, Jack.

JACK. Not really. Not in business.

LARRY. Jack?

JACK. Just look at the disk. That's all I'm saying.

LARRY. Put it on paper and I'll look at it, but I'm not making any promises other than that.

JACK. I'll have it for you before the end of today.

LARRY. Any other hassles?

JACK. Just these fucking Commanches.

LARRY. OK. Tell Norman to bring him in. (JACK *begins to move towards the door.*) Now, Jack. Listen to the way I handle this. If it works out, I want you to do the same thing with the others.

JACK. No problem. (*Pause.*) But listen, I'm not going on about it but I just want to say that I appreciate you giving me this

chance and everything, but it's just that I don't want to let
you down and that's why I've been working so hard on
these plans.

LARRY. You're doing great, Jack. But the reality is that
everything hinges on Alec. Not me, unfortunately.

JACK. I know, I know.

LARRY. Here's the way it is, the more votes a man like Alec
gets, the more power he gets. So he moves up. And if Alec
moves up, we all move up.

JACK. I hear what you're saying.

JACK *opens door, signals to* NORMAN *and* KYLE *then
returns to his seat.*

NORMAN *returns with* KYLE.

Sit down, kid.

KYLE. Don't call me kid.

JACK. I said Kyle. I didn't say kid.

NORMAN. Sit down, aul' hand.

KYLE *stares at* NORMAN. NORMAN *acts innocent.*

LARRY. Pull up a chair, Kyle.

KYLE (*does so and sits*). Where have you been?

LARRY. Where's your team?

KYLE. Waiting.

LARRY. What's the score?

KYLE. That's what I'm here to find out.

LARRY. Well, what's the feeling?

KYLE. What's your feeling?

LARRY. My feeling is that we're going through a difficult
transitional period.

NORMAN. Do you know what that means?

KYLE. Do you?

JACK. Norman!

JACK *indicates that* NORMAN *is to stay out of this conversation.* NORMAN *takes up a position at the door.*

LARRY. We're changing, Kyle. We're progressing.

KYLE. Who's we?

LARRY. Us. (KYLE *shakes his head.*) You don't think so?

JACK. But you don't know what everybody else thinks.

KYLE. I know what I think. I haven't changed.

LARRY. Maybe that's the problem.

KYLE. I don't want to change.

JACK. We all have to change, Kyle. Just like we all have to get older. It's natural.

LARRY. Kyle, whether you like it or not, things *have* changed. Whether I like it or not, things will never be the same again. Do you see what I'm saying?

KYLE. Are you going to back him up then?

LARRY. I don't know what you mean.

KYLE. Who's making all these decisions?

LARRY. The Command makes the decisions.

KYLE. When did the Command start getting involved in clubs?

LARRY (*confused*). What are you talking about?

KYLE. It's not that long ago me and my team were driving up that road out there with a truck full of beer and cigarettes. I don't remember anyone trying to stop us coming in then.

LARRY. Norman's only just started this new job, he was a bit over enthusiastic.

NORMAN. I just do what I'm told.

KYLE. What are we now – just shit like? Everything that we've done just doesn't count for shit any more. Is that the way it's going to be?

JACK. You've always been well looked after. Or you wouldn't have kept on doing things.

KYLE. I'm not talking to you.

LARRY. The way things are going to be Kyle is really up to yourself.

KYLE. How is it?

LARRY. Nothing's been set in stone. Everything is still up for grabs, do you know what I mean? You can either come on board or state your case. That's what I'm here for – to listen to you and to check that we're doing the right thing.

KYLE. Well you're not doing the right thing.

LARRY. In what way exactly?

KYLE. What you're doing with us is wrong.

JACK. When you do things right, you get rewarded. When you do things wrong therefore, it stands to reason that you have to be punished.

KYLE. If you interrupt me once more when I'm talking I'll go over that table and punish your face.

NORMAN. Do you want me to throw him out for threatening behaviour?

JACK. Does he have to do that, Kyle?

KYLE. If I was you I'd go and get my friends, Norman. 'Cause if I don't get a result here there's going to be threatening behaviour all over these floors.

LARRY. Settle down, Kyle. Take it easy.

JACK. You see, Larry. This is the problem.

LARRY. Talk to me, Kyle.

KYLE. I'm trying to.

LARRY. What would you like me to do for you?

KYLE. First of all I want this stupid ban lifted.

LARRY. What ban?

KYLE. The ban.

JACK. We had to ban two members of Kyle's team from the club for a short time.

LARRY. When did this happen?

JACK. They were getting out of hand.

LARRY. Sorry Kyle, I didn't know anything about this mate. Jack you'll have to scrap that immediately.

JACK. Only if I can have assurances of better behaviour.

LARRY. There is obviously a problem here, Jack. Let's get it sorted out now and I'm sure there'll be no further trouble. Am I right, Kyle?

KYLE. They started it.

LARRY. Well it's gone now. The ban's lifted.

KYLE. Good.

JACK. I can't really lift the ban on Freddie though. It only started last night.

LARRY. Jack?

JACK. I'm sorry, Larry, but I can't let him back in for a while at least.

LARRY. Why not?

JACK. No-one can handle him. He just causes too much trouble.

KYLE. I can sort that out, just like I did last night.

JACK. That was too late, the damage was done.

LARRY. Let's sort things out now, Jack.

KYLE. I can handle Freddie.

JACK. I've heard that from him before.

KYLE. Don't give me this attitude, Jack. I can handle him if you's agree to stop annoying him every two minutes.

JACK. He has to learn not to annoy everyone else.

LARRY. Let's make a deal then. What about this? Freddie's allowed back in the club only when he's with you. How's that sound?

KYLE. I don't know.

LARRY. That would only be temporary too. Until he proves himself to Jack.

KYLE. When's Jack going to prove himself to us?

LARRY. Jack's doing a fine job, Kyle.

JACK. Is this about the drink?

KYLE. No it's not about the drink. It's about attitude.

LARRY. What do you mean?

JACK. Someone has to explain to these fellas that the drink can't be all free all the time.

LARRY. Is that what the problem is?

KYLE. That's not the problem at all. (*To* JACK.) And you know it. (*To* LARRY.) But this is exactly what I mean.

LARRY. What is the problem then?

KYLE. I told you – attitude. Every time we come in here for a drink – all we get is this attitude.

LARRY. I don't know what that means.

NORMAN. Every time they come here, Larry. They cause trouble.

KYLE. Fuck up, Norman.

JACK. You see.

LARRY. Look! Kyle. Are you listening?

KYLE. Go ahead.

LARRY. I think I know what the problem is here.

KYLE. Him (*Jack*) and him (*Norman*).

JACK. And you's never did anything?

KYLE. I've done plenty. What have you done?

JACK. I'm running a business here.

KYLE. You're running a club. Our club.

JACK. It's not your club.

KYLE. It is our club. Isn't it, Larry?

LARRY. It's everybody's club.

JACK. But everybody can't enjoy it if we have the likes of Freddie in it.

KYLE. One more. One more fucking word.

LARRY. Kyle?

KYLE. Have we or have we not always done the business for you Larry? Answer me that.

LARRY. Of course you have.

KYLE. Whenever you called us in. Whenever something had to be done – who did it? Us. (*To* JACK.) That's right.

JACK. And you were rewarded.

KYLE. What's that supposed to mean?

JACK. It means what it means.

KYLE (*to* LARRY). You see Larry. (*To* JACK.) Do you think we did all this shit for you, Jack? Or for a few free pints of your shitty beer. Fuck you!

LARRY. There's no need for that.

NORMAN. Hey!

KYLE. Don't you fucking, 'Hey!' me.

JACK. You're just shooting yourself in the foot here, Kyle.

KYLE. Am I?

JACK. Yes you are. Keep going.

KYLE (*to* LARRY). This is what it's like. Every time. They just nag and nag and nag. It cracks me up, Larry.

LARRY. Well, let's talk it out. Do you want to go and have a drink – on me?

KYLE. I don't want any kind of drink. I'm not here to get something for free. And I'll talk to the lads about that too, although I think they deserve as much free drink as they want.

JACK. Well, we don't.

LARRY. Jack!

JACK. Sorry.

KYLE. Thank you. Anyway, here's the score. All we want is, obviously to be let back in – all of us. But better than that and because of what fuck-wit said, what I think would suit everybody would be if we could have a private area. How's that? Doesn't have to be a separate room, but just a place slightly more private and maybe a little bit more comfortable.

LARRY. I'm sure we can work something out, Kyle. (*To* JACK.) Couldn't we Jack?

Pause.

Jack!

JACK (*hesitation*). It would have to be a temporary arrangement until we could see how things go.

LARRY (*to* KYLE). Fair enough?

KYLE. Fair enough.

JACK. Fair enough.

Pause.

LARRY. Now listen, I've something else, I wanted to talk to you about. Now's as good a time as any. It could solve all our problems in one go. Are you going to listen?

KYLE. Go ahead.

LARRY. I need some men to do a job for me.

KYLE. What kind of job?

LARRY. There's been problems keeping some people on board. (*Chooses words carefully.*) People without the sense and the patience that you have. Renegades.

KYLE. What about them?

LARRY. They have to be dealt with, Kyle.

KYLE. What are you talking about?

LARRY. They won't listen. They won't do what they're told. They could jeopardise everything we're working for.

KYLE. What do you want me to do about it?

LARRY. I want you to bring them in.

KYLE. Fuck that.

LARRY. Kyle?

KYLE. No way.

LARRY. Think about it.

JACK. Maybe he's not up to it.

LARRY. I think he is.

KYLE. You want us to be a punishment team.

LARRY. Think about it like this. When you're fighting a war you need discipline. You need a chain of command.

JACK. We have that.

LARRY. And sometimes the Command decides to change our tactics or to try a different strategy. When they do that, unfortunately, some people get confused. Some people start doing their own thing as if they were the Command and others turn against the Command and start making accusations. These people are not Loyalists and they have to be sorted out. It's a difficult thing to do and it's a difficult thing to ask people to do, and that's why you're my first choice, Kyle. It's not like I'm asking you to kill anyone.

KYLE. Well you better not. I'm not killing Protestants.

LARRY. This is my point, Kyle. This is why I chose you. You're the obvious choice.

KYLE. I don't know Larry. I hate punishment squads. Everybody does.

LARRY. Kyle. (*Pause.*) You're just thinking about it in the wrong way. Punishment squads are very important, they do a dirty job, but a dirty job that has to be done.

KYLE. Fuck it, I'm not doing it.

LARRY. OK. Fair enough. But let me tell you this, if you don't do it, someone else has to do it. And that could be someone that you don't want to be doing something like that. Will you at least think it over? (KYLE *shakes his head.*) See someone might think that if you take that attitude, if you refuse to do this, maybe you have another plan of your own. Someone might even suggest that you are a renegade.

KYLE. I'm no renegade. And if anyone says I am I'll renegade their fucking head for them.

JACK. If that's true then you have to do what you're being told to do. That's how it works.

KYLE. I was just about to say yes and then he butted in, Larry.

LARRY. Jack, give me a minute here.

JACK. Sorry.

LARRY. I need your answer as soon as possible. We need to move fast. Start rounding them up before they can do any more damage.

KYLE. I've given you my answer, Larry.

LARRY. Then you tell me what I'm supposed to do. 'Cause I have a big fucking problem, Kyle. You know me. I would live and I would fucking die for Ulster, do you believe me when I say that?

KYLE. I do.

LARRY. Well then I want you to believe me when I tell you this. We're the Ulster Defence Association. We exist solely to defend Ulster. Now our leadership has told us that we've reached a point where we've to stand down or step back a bit. Ulster isn't under attack at the minute. So, there's nothing for us to defend against.

KYLE. I think there is.

LARRY. Well there you go, there's your first mistake. It's not up to us to think, Kyle. Do you see what I'm saying? We're not members of a fucking debating society. We're soldiers. Brought on board to do a job, not to think about it, not to ask questions but to follow orders because we are loyal. Loyal to Ulster, Loyal to the community – loyal to the chain of command.

KYLE. I am loyal. I do follow orders, I do, do what I'm told but all I'm saying to you is this . . . I don't want to do this. I'm better than this, I have more to offer than this.

LARRY. That's where you're wrong.

KYLE. What?

LARRY. There's nothing better than this. You've robbed a few banks, ripped off a mountain of cigarettes and beer and it's all good stuff, all hugely appreciated. But here's the thing, Kyle. Those days are over. And here's what's left for you,

you can sit in your own little area, drinking your fill and telling stories about the glory days every night for the rest of your life. Or you could try and bring those days back, do more jobs only keep the money for yourself but then you'd just be an ordinary criminal, a gangster, a villain. Do you understand?

KYLE. I don't have to do any of those.

LARRY. No, you don't. You could just walk away, wash your hands and in time all this will be forgotten. But this brings me back to your point. You've more to offer than that. (*Pause.*) You see, I could get any arsehole I wanted to do this. I could let them just pick their enemies, name them as renegades and fuck them up. I could just sit in my house and leave them to get on with it, but I'm not like that. When I'm given a job to do I want to do it to the best of my abilities. That's why I need good men around me, to help me do it properly. Think about it, think about what it means, think about where it puts you in everybody's minds. Not arseholes who don't understand what has to be done, but the people that count, the people who matter. They're going to see you do this and they're going to remember you. Know what I mean? Think about that. (*Pause.*) Look, I had hoped that it wouldn't come to this. I had hoped that somehow I could explain it better to you. But you're just sitting there. And that disappoints me.

KYLE. I'm not here to disappoint you, I'm here to help.

LARRY. Then help me do this. Help me stop people from fucking it all up for us. Help me to help people understand what we're doing here and what we have to do to help our politicians make this thing fucking work. Don't make me order you to do this – that wouldn't be right. Just tell me that you'll try to convince the others, that'll do me.

KYLE. And what if I can't?

JACK. Then they'll be the first ones we want you to bring in.

LARRY. Jack, shut the fuck up! (LARRY *slaps* JACK.) He's joking! But the thing is, Kyle. If they don't come on board and they don't do what has to be done – what does that say about them?

KYLE. I hear you.

LARRY. I mean, they're your team and that carries a certain amount of weight with me, but I have to tell you that all I'm hearing from people and I don't mean just people like Jack, I mean everybody. All I hear from everybody is that your team are trouble. Dougie and Mac can be a very dangerous duo and Freddie, I mean for fuck sake, Kyle. Sometimes it's difficult to work out who the fuck Freddie is fighting against.

KYLE. I'll sort that out.

LARRY. Make sure you do, I need everybody on board or out of circulation.

KYLE *considers.*

KYLE. OK. But here's the way it goes. If I buy what you're selling, if I agree to this. Then the only people we'll be doing are the renegades, right?

LARRY. Absolutely.

KYLE. And a renegade is a person who doesn't follow orders as described by you in your little Chain of Command speech, yeah? (LARRY *nods.*) Then tell him (*Jack*) to stay the fuck off our backs for good and make it an order and if he doesn't obey it then he's a renegade and he's brought in and well . . . (*To* JACK.) Get the picture Jack?

LARRY. Get the man a drink, Norman. And let's see if we can find an area that would suit him and his team.

NORMAN *leaves immediately.* LARRY *urges* KYLE *to follow and they leave* JACK. JACK *returns to work.*

Scene Five

Living room. Evening. FREDDIE *enters the living room and changes the tape on the ghetto blaster. When* SANDRA *arrives he is painting the skirting board.*

FREDDIE. Did you get talking to him?

SANDRA. No, I had to go on. I couldn't keep my Ma waiting outside any longer.

FREDDIE. Well, did he get talking to anybody, do you know?

SANDRA. Your guess is as good as mine.

FREDDIE. Was he all right like? About me I mean.

SANDRA. I don't know, Freddie.

FREDDIE. Fucked up, didn't I?

SANDRA. I don't think you did.

FREDDIE. He does but. (*Stops painting and stands. Waits.*)

SANDRA. What?

FREDDIE. Do you think he would've done it?

SANDRA. Done what?

FREDDIE. Me? Know at the end – when I had Norman by the throat and he came at me with the cue. Do you think he would've used it on me?

SANDRA. I wouldn't like to think so.

FREDDIE. I thought he would. That's why I let Norman go.

SANDRA. I hate that wanker Norman.

FREDDIE. I know what you mean. He's got the sort of face that you never get tired of kicking. And he's a dirty fucker too. Bastard caught me a couple of crackers, did you see them?

SANDRA. I did. And I saw fucking Paul hitting you as well.

FREDDIE. I don't remember that. (*Pause.*) I remember hitting Norman once with the cue and Paul came flying over from the bar and two of his mates jumped up from their table and headed for me as well. I could see them out of the corner of my eye, I just thought to myself – 'Here we fucking go'.

FREDDIE *enjoys telling the story, complete with all the actions from his point of view.* SANDRA *clearly enjoys it too.*

I just started swinging the cue about – smashing things, making sure no-one could get at me. But, you know when they were all standing off trying to talk me down, I realised that the thing about it was, you think the cue's a good thing because it stops them coming in on you but then you can't get hurting anybody – so in a way it's a bit of a waste of time.

SANDRA. I was wondering why you threw it at the barman.

FREDDIE. Then again the good thing about swinging the cue was that it gave me a good look at everybody – you need that like. Mistake was I thought Norman was scared and the guy from the table was the one to worry about so I concentrated on hitting him and that's when your man got me a couple of crackers. Bang – Bang! Two weekers.

SANDRA. And then you went fucking mental. I thought you were going to kill somebody.

FREDDIE. No, it wouldn't have come to that. That's just a reaction to the pain and more to the annoyance of letting that cunt get a dig in, you know. But he paid for it and he would've paid a lot more if Kyle hadn't decided to get involved.

SANDRA. I couldn't believe that.

FREDDIE. Ah fuck it, forget about it.

SANDRA. I can't. I'm very fucking worried about it.

FREDDIE. Don't be.

SANDRA. It was bad enough when he took their side against Dougie and Mac.

FREDDIE. Dougie and Mac fucked up but.

SANDRA. How did they?

FREDDIE. I don't know – Kyle said they did.

SANDRA. You were there, did you think they did?

FREDDIE. I was fucked, I had drank too much. I can only go on what Kyle said.

SANDRA. Well, Kyle seems to be saying the same thing about you now.

FREDDIE. I know, I fucked up too.

SANDRA. I don't think you did. Same as I don't think Dougie and Mac did either. I think it's Kyle.

FREDDIE. How did Kyle fuck up?

SANDRA *closes in on him.*

SANDRA. Think about it. Think about the way he's been getting on. Have you noticed anything about him recently?

FREDDIE. I don't know. I fucking . . . sometimes I just seem to be on my own.

SANDRA. Keep going.

FREDDIE. Not just with Kyle. But that was the latest one. Like last night when I got home I just lay in bed thinking about it. Me and him always seemed to be on the same wavelength. Mine was maybe a wee bit more, you know, in your face. His maybe . . . better thought out or something but after this – Fuck it, it's not just with him. It seems to be with everybody. Take a look around. Have you been watching TV lately?

SANDRA. He never has it off the bloody football.

FREDDIE. Fuck football – this is serious stuff.

SANDRA. You don't need to tell me that, Freddie. I know that.

FREDDIE. Does Kyle know it but?

SANDRA. This is it Freddie, this is my problem. I don't think he does. It's as if he's forgotten everything. Do you know what I'm saying? Can you remember things like . . . properly? Can you remember all the things that we've talked about? And all the things that we've done. (*Pause.*) When Kyle asked me out, he told me he was doing a job in Gallaghers. I says, I'm not going with a dickhead, factory worker baleeks. And he says, I'm not *working* in Gallaghers, I'm doing a *job* in Gallaghers.

FREDDIE *laughs and stops painting.*

FREDDIE. Do you know what I remember most about that job? He talked about you all day, put my fucking head away he did. We had to do the van at Trooper's Lane. Half a million cigarettes, fucking brilliant. Blocked it in and

fucked the driver and his mate out and away we went. The
whole time I was panicking because your man's head
wasn't on the job. Next thing I know he's turning into a
garage. I says, what are you doing? He says, I told Sandra
I'd get her some cigarettes. I says we've half a fucking
million of them in the back. And he says, she doesn't smoke
Gallaghers. Fuck me!

SANDRA. Those days were great.

FREDDIE. Fucking right they were. And do you know why?
Because they were simple. Straight forward. Everybody
knew where they were. Not like now. We used to walk into
that club and every fucker in the place would be patting us
on the back and yelling our names out – the drink would
just flow all night. And then, all of a sudden . . .

Stops.

SANDRA. Everything changed.

FREDDIE. Too fucking right it did. (*Pause.*) Well fuck change
that's what I say. Why can't everything stay the same.

SANDRA. Has *he* changed, Freddie? Is that what it is?
(*Pause.*) He sits there day after day and he sees it just like
we do and he does nothing. He might say something about
the BBC having an Ireland correspondent and he would
shout at the TV (*Acts* KYLE.) 'It's *Northern* Ireland.' And
then he'd do a wee rant about fucking BBC Northern
Ireland being run by fenians, but that's it – a few fucking
yells at the TV (*Acting* KYLE.) '*British* Broadcasting
Corporation.' That's the height of his involvement these
days. Some fucking Super Prod he turned out to be. That's
why I need you to talk to him.

FREDDIE. He won't listen.

SANDRA. We're going to have to make him listen. We're
going to have to make everybody start listening.

FREDDIE. How?

SANDRA. I don't fucking know. You tell me.

FREDDIE. The only way to get people to listen is . . . We need
to *do* something. We don't need any more talking, we need

to start doing. Something big. Something that'll get every-body sitting up and taking notice.

SANDRA. Like what but?

FREDDIE. What am I the fucking brains of Britain all of a fucking sudden?

SANDRA watches as FREDDIE talks, he moves to the pasting table and picks up the paste and begins to check it.

FREDDIE. Will we do this wall before he gets here?

SANDRA. I don't know about papering today, I'm knackered.

FREDDIE. I'll tell you what, you keep the tea coming and I'll have it done in two ticks.

FREDDIE lifts a roll of paper and opens it. SANDRA closes in again and helps him measure the paper against the wall. After FREDDIE marks it for length SANDRA goes to the kitchen and FREDDIE places it on the table, cuts it and pastes it before SANDRA returns. When KYLE enters carrying a six pack of beers FREDDIE and SANDRA are hanging the patterned bottom half of the wallpaper. KYLE sets four tins down and carries two with him.

KYLE. How's it going?

FREDDIE and SANDRA continue working.

SANDRA. Hope you're not expecting any fucking dinner.

KYLE (*ignoring SANDRA*). Don't be knocking yourself out just 'cause of me, Freddie.

FREDDIE. I'm dead on, I want to get this done.

SANDRA. Don't fucking ignore me.

KYLE. Isn't that lovely to come home to, Freddie?

SANDRA. If you don't like it, don't come fucking home.

After finishing measuring another strip SANDRA goes into the kitchen. FREDDIE begins to paste the next strip. KYLE sets a tin of beer beside FREDDIE.

FREDDIE. I'm getting a cup of tea.

FREDDIE keeps working. KYLE watches him.

KYLE. It's looking good, Freddie. Very good.

FREDDIE. It's easy enough when you know what you're doing.

KYLE. Stop and have a wee break.

FREDDIE. I'm all right.

KYLE. Come on mate, what do you say we down these and go to the club?

SANDRA. What for – to let them throw us out again?

FREDDIE. Fuck the club.

KYLE. Fuck the club?

FREDDIE. Fuck Larry. Fuck Jack. Fuck them all.

KYLE. They're not my type.

SANDRA *returns with two cups of tea. She gives one to* FREDDIE.

SANDRA. You could have fooled us.

FREDDIE (*smiles*). From now on I'll be drinking somewhere else. Somewhere with a better class of people.

KYLE. Freddie, there is nowhere else. What are you getting on like this for?

SANDRA. What way are we getting on?

KYLE. Well, (*To* SANDRA.) you're just your usual annoying self, but I came back hoping to talk to my mate.

SANDRA. And what are you, just your usual dickhead self?

KYLE. Do you want to talk or not, Freddie?

FREDDIE. Fuck talk.

KYLE. Well what do you want to do? (*Waits. No reply.*) What do you want to do, Freddie?

FREDDIE (*searches for words*). Fuck it.

KYLE. Come on, help me out here big man. What's going on? (*Points at* FREDDIE's *head.*) In there?

FREDDIE. Nothing.

KYLE. No change there, then.

FREDDIE. Away and fuck, Kyle! Will you?

KYLE. That's lovely.

SANDRA. What do you want, Kyle?

KYLE (*hesitates, glances at* SANDRA). I want to get things sorted with Freddie.

FREDDIE. Like you did last night?

KYLE. That's part of what I want to talk to you about.

FREDDIE *begins to paste another strip of paper.*

SANDRA. What do you have to say for yourself?

KYLE. We've got problems, Freddie.

SANDRA. Hey! Deal with this first.

KYLE. I'm trying to talk to Freddie here.

FREDDIE (*to* SANDRA). Forget about it. (*Pause.*) Give me a hand with this.

SANDRA *helps* FREDDIE *hang another strip.* KYLE *waits.*

KYLE. So what do you say, Freddie?

FREDDIE. I say you're right. We've got problems.

KYLE. Well, are you going to tell me what you think they are.

FREDDIE. If you don't know what they are, then you're one of them. (*Points into* KYLE's *face.*).

KYLE. Don't point in my face.

FREDDIE (*still pointing*). So, should I be worried about you too?

KYLE. Don't. (*Pushes* FREDDIE's *hand away.*).

FREDDIE. Deals. Do you remember? Everybody has a deal. What's your deal? (*Points into* KYLE's *face again*).

KYLE. Stop sticking your finger in my fucking face, will you?

FREDDIE. I'll point my fucking finger wherever to fuck I want. What's your deal? (*Pushes his finger into* KYLE's *face.* KYLE *pushes it away and stands up.*)

KYLE. Fuck you.

FREDDIE. Let's go. You and me.

Pause. FREDDIE *waits,* KYLE *turns away.* FREDDIE *laughs.*

KYLE. You drive me crazy, Freddie. Do you know that? You're a crazy bastard.

FREDDIE. Don't try to butter me up.

KYLE (*reaches* FREDDIE *a beer and struggles to speak*). Freddie, listen to me.

FREDDIE. Why should I listen to you, when you won't listen to me?

SANDRA. You won't listen to anybody.

FREDDIE. Tell me this. See when it says on TV progress has been made – what does that mean?

KYLE. I don't know what you mean.

SANDRA. You know fine rightly what he means.

FREDDIE. I'll tell you what it means. It means they've moved us closer to a United Ireland.

KYLE. Don't talk shit.

SANDRA. Don't you talk shit.

KYLE. Will you fuck up I'm trying to talk to Freddie here?

SANDRA. Don't tell me to fuck up or I'll lift that tin of paint and bury it in your head.

FREDDIE. Fuck it! I'm going to head on. Thanks for the tea, Sandra. I'll be back tomorrow and we'll finish this off.

SANDRA. Are you sure?

FREDDIE. I'll just tidy this last wee bit up and then I'm out of here.

SANDRA (*to* KYLE). Try being a bit more grateful.

KYLE. How can I? Every time I open my mouth you jump all over me.

SANDRA. Freddie's worked his arse off here.

Pause. SANDRA *begins to help* FREDDIE *clear things away.*

KYLE. Let me help you finish that and then we'll have a wee beer and I'll tell you the good news.

SANDRA. What good news?

KYLE. I was going to tell you before you started slabbering.

SANDRA. Just tell us.

KYLE. I got the ban lifted we can go down the club and celebrate right now if you want or we can snub them and drink here.

SANDRA. Dougie and Mac and all?

KYLE (*nods*). Oh yeah. And do you want to know what else I got for us?

SANDRA. What?

KYLE. Our own little area.

FREDDIE. Where abouts?

KYLE. Near the back.

SANDRA. What will we do then? (*To* FREDDIE.) Do you want to go down Freddie?

FREDDIE. Is this place big enough for the whole team?

SANDRA. And their wives? Or girlfriends?

KYLE. Oh yeah.

SANDRA. Then why don't we get everybody now and make a night of it?

KYLE. Why don't the three of us just go? We can bring everybody else tomorrow night.

SANDRA. What do you say Freddie? It's brilliant, isn't it?

FREDDIE. It's good.

KYLE. You see, when there's a problem that needs sorted what do you do? You call for me.

KYLE *passes beers around.*

FREDDIE. Cheers! I never doubted you for a second.

KYLE. Unbelievable.

SANDRA (*to* KYLE). How'd you do it?

FREDDIE. Who's in hospital?

KYLE. Nobody.

FREDDIE. Not even Jack?

KYLE. There was no need.

SANDRA. Why did he just wet himself and lift the ban straight away?

KYLE. No. We came to an understanding.

FREDDIE. With your fist in his face, right?

KYLE. No. We just worked it out.

SANDRA. What way?

KYLE. We talked.

FREDDIE (*worried*). You didn't ask them nicely, did you?

SANDRA. Did you Kyle?

KYLE. I got it sorted.

FREDDIE. Did you get down on your knees and beg?

SANDRA. Did you suck some dick?

KYLE. Hey! (*Stands.*) I did what I did and it's sorted so do you want to come down for a drink or not?

FREDDIE. No.

KYLE. You don't fancy it now?

FREDDIE. I like the idea of the snub better.

KYLE. Why?

FREDDIE. Just the kind of guy I am.

KYLE. What, stupid?

SANDRA. Don't start again.

FREDDIE. You's go down if you's want. But I won't be asking people to let me drink in our club.

KYLE. What do you want me to do?

FREDDIE. I don't want you to do anything, Kyle.

KYLE. Well then what is it, Freddie?

FREDDIE. It's just not the way it should be. They should have come here and asked us to come back to their shitty wee club.

SANDRA. And they should have apologised too.

KYLE. Wise up. People don't apologise to you because you busted up their place, now do they?

SANDRA. That's not the point.

FREDDIE. He knows it's not the point, Sandra. (*To* KYLE.) Don't you?

KYLE. Freddie?

FREDDIE. I'm out of here.

KYLE. Freddie wait, talk to me.

FREDDIE. Fuck talk.

> FREDDIE *leaves.* SANDRA *paces.*

SANDRA. I never thought I'd see the day you would do something like this.

KYLE. What have I done? Apart from just trying to help everybody.

SANDRA. I suppose I was really just kidding myself. I could see it coming a mile.

KYLE. Listen Sandra.

SANDRA. You're pathetic.

KYLE (*more determined*). Listen!

SANDRA. Go.

KYLE. I need your help here.

SANDRA. What with?

KYLE. We have to talk to Freddie before things get worse.

SANDRA. Freddie's not the problem.

KYLE. He is, Sandra.

SANDRA. Fuck this.

KYLE. No we can't fuck this – this isn't just about Freddie – this isn't just about the club – this is about everything. Me, you, Joe – your Ma. Every fucking thing.

SANDRA. How is it?

KYLE. Because it is. Think about it. Things have been going bad with us, with Freddie, with everybody, ever since this fucking process started and we were told to stop doing what we do and all the money stopped coming in because of it. Am I right or wrong?

SANDRA. This isn't about money.

KYLE. I didn't say it's about money. But money's part of it. We need money. Money to get this place done up properly – to pay your Ma off – to give Joe a better life – to get the car sorted out. This is about all that. This is about money for Freddie, for his place, for his Ma. Dougie, Mac, wives, girlfriends. We all need money, Sandra. We might not like it but it's the way it is.

SANDRA. Well if it's just about money why not do a job and get some money?

KYLE. Because of what I'm trying to tell you. It's not just about money. It's about Loyalty. Freddie says he's a Loyalist, well if that's true, then Freddie has to come on board, do you understand? There's nothing to do. There's no jobs to be done at the minute. Not the jobs that we normally do.

SANDRA. Then what are you going to do?

KYLE. I'm going to be loyal. Loyal to you, loyal to my family, loyal to my country. How far do you want me to go?

SANDRA. I want you to go as far as to get to the fucking point.

KYLE. Well, the point is, I've sorted something with Larry. I've got us into the club – I've got us our own little area and I've got everybody off our backs and I mean everybody. But that still leaves us with a big problem.

SANDRA. Which is?

KYLE. Not everybody's on board.

SANDRA. On board what?

KYLE. OK not on board – in line.

SANDRA. Well that clears that up.

KYLE. Look Sandra there has always been a command structure and it's a structure you can't fuck with, do you know what I'm saying?

SANDRA. I'm listening.

KYLE. Decisions have been made. Now I don't like those decisions – same as Freddie – same as a lot of people but that doesn't mean we can go off and do our own thing anyway. We can't. We have to do what we're told.

SANDRA. And what have you been told?

KYLE. I've been told to make sure everybody's on board, in line.

SANDRA. And what if they're not?

KYLE. Then we have to do them.

SANDRA. I knew you were going to say that. You're a fucking punishment squad, aren't you? That's what you're telling me, isn't it? That's what all this shite is about.

KYLE. We're not a punishment squad.

SANDRA. Well, it fucking sounds like it to me.

KYLE. Punishment squads do housebreakers and glue sniffers – what I'm talking about doing here is renegades – bad men. And it would be a one off.

SANDRA. What about Freddie? If he doesn't come on board are you going to do him? Will that be a one off or are you going to do all our friends?

KYLE. That's why I need your help.

SANDRA. Fuck me!

KYLE. Think about it. We had three of our own team barred from our club. If we don't do this, how easy is it going to be for someone to point the finger at us and say we're the fucking problem? Think about that.

SANDRA. I can't listen to this.

KYLE. Well what do you want me to do – get a job sweeping the roads. That's all I'm qualified for – or maybe digging fucking ditches. I can't do that.

SANDRA. But you could be a member of a punishment squad?

KYLE. I'm fucked here. Do you think I want to do this? Do you think this is my idea. It might come as a fucking surprise to you but I'm completely fucked here. This is it, this is the only option I have and it's the only option Freddie and the boys will have too. At least with me they'll have a chance of making it through this.

SANDRA. Do you think so?

KYLE. It's fact. What if they got a cunt like Davies to do it, huh? He hates Dougie. He would have Dougie done before you knew what the fuck was happening. What if they picked Big Heck Henderson. He hates all of us.

SANDRA. Fuck him.

KYLE. We can't fuck him. This is going to happen no matter what we do. If we want to make sure it's done properly, then we have to do it ourselves. You can't walk away, let it happen and then complain about it afterwards. Too late. We have to get in at the beginning and see it through to the end. It's the only way.

SANDRA *thinks,* KYLE *studies her – waiting.*

KYLE. Do you want a beer?

SANDRA *nods,* KYLE *brings the beer over to her.*

They sit. They drink. They stare at each other.

Interval.

Scene Six

Punishment room. Morning.

LARRY *and* ALEC *are sitting at the table.* NORMAN *arrives.*

NORMAN. I've just brought Kyle over. Jack's with him.

ALEC. I have to get going.

LARRY. When you see Alec leave bring him up.

NORMAN. OK.

NORMAN *leaves.*

ALEC. Listen, I hope there's no hard feelings between us. I did my best for you.

LARRY. Can't ask any more than that.

ALEC. And I'll keep at them, Larry. I mean it. I want you in. I think you could have a big impact in politics.

LARRY. Just tell me something, Alec. What was the main problem?

ALEC. Larry, sometimes you can be the right man at the wrong time, you know.

LARRY. That's no good to me, Alec.

ALEC. Well, maybe this is something to think about. Maybe you could lose some of this sympathy you have for these young men. That doesn't mean you have to stop caring. It means, in fact, that you have to care more about them. But you also have to look after yourself too. Distance yourself – sometimes.

LARRY. Distance myself. I think I've done a bit more than just distance myself from them, Alec. I mean did you talk to the top men, did you tell them about everything I'm doing?

ALEC. Of course I did, but you have to understand, Larry. We're a small party and a small party can only take care of a small amount of people. Do you know what I mean?

LARRY. I never asked to be taken care of. I want to help.
I want to contribute.

ALEC. And you will – in time.

LARRY is disappointed.

Look, mate. Next time I'll push harder and you know, when
this mess is sorted out and things are running smooth, that'll
all be in your favour. I don't see how they can keep you out
if you do a good job with this.

LARRY. Maybe they're right, Alec. Maybe I'm not cut out for
politics.

ALEC. Would that be such a bad thing?

*Silence. LARRY considers ALEC's statement and searches
for the truth in his eyes.*

Well, it's your decision. No-one can force you to stand for
election.

LARRY. No.

ALEC. I'll talk to you tomorrow when I call by to pick up that
donation you were telling me about. Now, that is something
else that will always be in your favour.

LARRY. Good.

ALEC. I'll see you then.

*ALEC leaves. NORMAN returns, followed by JACK and
KYLE. LARRY greets them.*

JACK. Did you say anything to Alec?

LARRY. No.

KYLE. What was he doing here?

LARRY. Just talking.

KYLE. That's all he's good at.

JACK. So, he doesn't know.

LARRY. No. We need time to try and sort something out. He
didn't need to know.

KYLE. What about?

LARRY. We've got another problem, Kyle.

KYLE. Wouldn't be like you.

JACK. Can we take this down to my office, Larry?

LARRY. No.

JACK (*to* KYLE). Where have you been all night?

KYLE. In bed.

JACK. Can you prove that?

KYLE. Just ask your wife.

NORMAN. What did you say?

LARRY. Fellas!

NORMAN. Did you hear what he said to Jack?

LARRY. Settle down.

KYLE. What's the problem?

JACK. Somebody held up the club.

KYLE. Seriously?

LARRY. Tell him the story Jack.

KYLE. No, no.

JACK. What?

KYLE. Not, the old, I was on my own, working late, when four masked men busted in and robbed the place, ploy.

JACK. Not quite. And not funny either.

NORMAN. There was only two.

KYLE. Only two? But they were masked though? I got that part right, yeah?

JACK. Yeah.

KYLE. And you think you might know who it was, right Jack?

JACK. I've a good idea.

NORMAN. Your mate.

KYLE. You're very predictable.

LARRY. Tell him what he was wearing.

JACK. Leather jacket, blue jeans. White T-shirt.

KYLE. Was it a clean one?

JACK. Don't play games here. I'm on the level with this.

KYLE. You fuck with me Jack and you'll be on the level permanently.

JACK. He's threatening me again.

KYLE. Yeah I am.

LARRY. Kyle, this is serious. Freddie really has robbed the club.

NORMAN. We want to know if the other guy was you.

KYLE. Well it fucking wasn't, all right?

They wait, each man checking the reactions and thought processes of the others.

LARRY. Kyle's word is good enough for me. (*Pause.*) Now Kyle, I need to know if you're going to help us here.

KYLE. I'll talk to him.

LARRY. I want to talk to him too.

KYLE. OK.

NORMAN. So do I.

KYLE (*to* NORMAN). But first, I have a couple of questions for you.

NORMAN. What like?

KYLE. You're the new Head of Security. So, what the fuck were you doing when this all happened?

JACK. One had a crow-bar.

NORMAN. I didn't!

KYLE. Are you telling me someone robbed this club with a crow-bar? I think you need better security, Larry.

LARRY. Are you applying for the job?

NORMAN. Fuck you! I just opened the door, saw two people, saw the crow-bar and the next thing I remember was Jack bringing me round.

KYLE. That brings me to you Jack?

JACK. What about me?

KYLE. You've turned the place around, you're always going on about how much work you've put in to it. It must hurt to just hand over those profits at the end of every month.

JACK. What are you trying to say?

KYLE. Couple of years ago a man came to me with a plan to rob that club.

JACK. Was it Freddie?

NORMAN. Case closed, Larry.

JACK (*to* KYLE). Keep going, you're digging your own grave.

KYLE. Larry knows all about this. (*To* LARRY.) Don't you Larry?

LARRY. Make your point.

KYLE. Put the money in a bag, mess up your hair and your suit. Maybe give Norman here a few digs. He's a big man, he can take it and cuts and bruises look good. The Police will come in, look around, armed robbery very evident, no clues etc, etc, case closed. And you just keep that money. The club claims the insurance and everybody is happy. (*To* LARRY.) Do you remember that plan, Larry?

LARRY. Of course I do.

KYLE. You could tear the arse out of it and put in for compensation, if you want. Maybe even go for medical retirement. (*To* JACK.) How's those nerves Jack?

JACK. I don't have to stand here and listen to this.

KYLE. You have to listen to this though. If that's the deal, that's the deal, I can play with it, but let's just leave Freddie out of it. We don't need anybody to take the fall. We never did in the past.

LARRY. This is not the deal this time, Kyle.

JACK. As hard as it is for you to believe, this place was robbed last night. And I'm one hundred per cent sure it was Freddie who did it. I recognised his shape, his voice, everything. It was him.

KYLE. What kind of money are we talking about?

JACK. Thirty five.

KYLE. Thirty five what?

NORMAN. Thirty five B and H, what the fuck do you think?

JACK. Thousand, Kyle.

LARRY. The man who just left here needs a lot of money for his next campaign. I promised him I'd do my best. I did and now it's all been fucked away on me. And I can't afford to let the people who did this get away with it. I want them and I want that money. Now, you know me Kyle, I don't care how I get it back or what state I leave those people in once I get it back from them, so help me, help them and help yourself.

JACK. And don't think you're above suspicion. I still want to know where you were.

KYLE. Jack, just you think about this. You're accusing my best mate of doing this. And you're the only one who says it was him. So you better hope we get a confession or we get more proof. Because if things go belly up and I find myself back here talking to you. You're really fucked. Think about it.

Scene Seven

Private Office. Morning.

NORMAN *and* JACK *enter the office.* NORMAN *is carrying a tray of drinks.* JACK *sits behind his desk and begins to go over some accounts.*

NORMAN. When will they be here?

JACK. Soon. Very soon.

NORMAN. We'll just wait then.

JACK. Yes, Norman.

> NORMAN *begins to whistle, this eventually disturbs*
> JACK*'s concentration.* JACK *stares at* NORMAN.
> NORMAN *finally realises and stops whistling. They wait.*

NORMAN. Can I ask you a question, Jack?

JACK. What?

NORMAN. Why do you keep going over and over the same pages?

JACK. It's just part of my job.

NORMAN. I know that, but I was just wondering why you keep changing the figures. I mean, where do you get all that from?

JACK. I told you Norman, it's my job.

NORMAN. Well it just strikes me that, you know, you said that we were all going legit from now on.

JACK. We are.

NORMAN. But . . .

JACK. Norman! I'm busy here. We are about to have the most important meeting of our careers and we're 35,000 pounds down. So excuse me for being a little bit unsettled about it.

NORMAN (*hesitates*). That's why I thought I would ask you.

JACK. Go then, get it all off your chest.

NORMAN. You said we were going to be doing everything by the books and I wanted to know if that was still the same plan.

JACK. Of course it is.

NORMAN. Well then why are you changing those figures? Even I know that what you're writing down isn't right.

JACK. This is business Norman. And in business there are things that are difficult to explain.

NORMAN. Well if I'm going to get anywhere I'm going to need to know these things, so like Larry's said to me, all I have to do is watch you.

JACK. Larry told you to watch me?

NORMAN. More than once.

JACK. What way, watch me?

NORMAN. Watch what you do and learn about all this.

JACK. What for?

NORMAN. So as I can take over.

JACK (*smiles*). Right.

NORMAN. So, are you going to explain all this to me or what?

JACK (*considers*). Think of it like this. What I'm doing here is juggling numbers. Sometimes money can get lost somewhere, receipts can go missing. People get careless.

NORMAN. A couple of the barmen are at it too. I just thought I'd mention that.

JACK. That's part of it as well, but Norman the main thing is that these are little white lies. Do you understand what I'm saying?

NORMAN. And would claiming the dole not just be a little white lie, then?

JACK. I told you about that Norman.

NORMAN. I was just thinking.

JACK. Listen to me. Take our barmen, like you just said, they're all at it, right?

NORMAN. Do you want me to do something about it?

JACK. No, and I'll tell you why not. I know what they're doing, they're stealing from me, but that's why I pay them less and that's why when it comes to this I juggle these figures and everything seems normal and everybody is satisfied. They think they're being clever and getting away with it and it keeps them happy. I know that they won't ever tear the arse out of it and that keeps me happy. Do you get it?

NORMAN. I don't steal from you, Jack.

JACK. I know and that's why I look after you and that's why I don't want you to put yourself in trouble by trying to claim the dole.

NORMAN. But what if . . . ?

ALEC *and* LARRY *arrive.* JACK *gets up instantly and urges* NORMAN, *who finally shows* ALEC *to a seat.* ALEC *ignores the seat and begins pacing around the room.* LARRY *takes* JACK's *seat and* JACK *stands nervously between them.*

JACK. Will I start, Larry?

LARRY. OK, Alec?

ALEC. Go ahead.

JACK. My figures show that we had slightly under 36 grand in the floor safe and as the police pointed out there was a few quid in the tills but that's still there because these boys came for this money and this money only. As far as the police are concerned, by the way, they think we lost a little less than five. And they also think I was unable to identify any of them.

NORMAN. I just said exactly what Jack told me to say.

JACK. Norman. (*To* ALEC.) I recognised one of them.

ALEC. Who was it?

JACK. It was a fella called Freddie. He was wearing a mask and all, but I know it was him.

ALEC. What about the other guy?

JACK. No idea.

NORMAN. But Freddie won't be long in telling us as soon as we get him in here.

LARRY. So what do you think, Alec?

ALEC. You promised me that money, Larry.

LARRY. And you promised me something too.

ALEC. There was nothing more I could do about that.

LARRY. And what could I do about this?

ALEC. Find him and get it back.

LARRY. I intend to.

NORMAN. We'll get him just as soon as somebody says the word.

ALEC. I know you can get him, anybody can get him but what about the money.

LARRY. That'll be harder.

JACK. I think he'll still have it.

NORMAN. Maybe not it all but most of it.

LARRY. But whether he'll give it up or not, I don't know.

ALEC. This isn't blackmail, is it Larry? Because if it is, it's a waste of time.

JACK. What are you implying?

ALEC. It just seems funny how there wasn't a problem with the money last night and then when I tell you about how my party's executive turned down my proposal to bring you on board suddenly . . . Suddenly out of the blue my big fat donation, as promised by you two days ago, has gone missing. Now, that's what I call a big fucking coincidence.

LARRY. Alec, I didn't take the fucking money. Get those sort of thoughts out of your head.

JACK. It definitely wasn't him. I would have recognised him too.

NORMAN. Unless you were in on it too, Jack. If you see what he means. (*Pause.*) Remember what Kyle said about his idea.

JACK. Forget about what Kyle said.

ALEC. What did Kyle say?

NORMAN. He was just telling us about somebody having this idea to rob the club. But it wouldn't really be robbed, it would be a ploy, know what I mean?

LARRY. Jack here was brought in to knock all that sort of behaviour on the head, Alec.

JACK. And I've done it, until now but who would ever have thought someone would actually rob us?

NORMAN. Apart from us, ourselves. (*Quickly.*) I don't mean you Jack. (*Points at* ALEC.) It's him! If you follow what he's thinking, that's what it means. (*To* ALEC.) I'm not getting at you, I'm just saying, isn't that what you mean?

ALEC. I need that money, Larry. It's essential to my campaign. I'm supposed to be touring America again. Do you realise how important to Ulster it is, that people like me represent us at the very highest level? How are the Yanks supposed to know what's going on, from our point of view, if there's no-one available to tell them? This is vital, if we are to maintain our high profile as serious political representatives. We have to stay in the right places, we have to be seen by the right people. And when we are seen we have to fit the bill and that bill costs money.

JACK. I understand exactly what you're saying.

ALEC. We're talking about serious suits, serious style, serious accommodation and serious transportation. Do you know what I'm saying? Five star hotels, top class restaurants all cost money. We can't turn up to dinner with American businessmen in our jeans and an aul' t-shirt. We can't grab fish and chips and head down the pub for a few pints and a bit of a laugh. This isn't fucking ejits wearing masks, burning cars, blocking roads and singing 'God Save the Queen' round a bonfire with a crate a beer each. This is the future.

LARRY. Let me tell you what this is, Alec. This is me. This is – it! (*Pause*). Jamesy's Da was a good friend of mine, when he died I took that boy under my wing.

ALEC. Who the fuck is Jamesy?

LARRY. Jamesy had a talent for Chemistry, he was doing 'A' levels.

ALEC. What has he to do with this?

NORMAN. We done him over.

ALEC. Was he the other guy?

LARRY. We don't know who the other guy was.

ALEC. Well, find out and when you do – I want the both of them done properly.

LARRY. Like Jamesy, you mean.

ALEC (*more serious*). Who the fuck is this Jamesy character?

LARRY. Jamesy is a young fella I encouraged every step of the way. Every faltering, fucking step. I got him books, I persuaded him to join me, us, in our campaign. All he was ever fucking interested in was a wee girl called Linda something. I talked to him night after night. Drink after drink. I turned him from a boy to a man. He came to me before with his plan about how we could plant bombs and grind Dublin to a halt. Just a few tiny details to sort out. I told him he'd get there, if he just kept at it. And he did. And then the goal posts were moved and I was told that I had to bring him in with a hood over his head and bash the fuck out of his legs. He might not walk again. Of course before I laid a finger on him, I tried to turn around all the things I had put in his head. I tried to double talk him. He wouldn't listen, it seems I was too good the first time round. Well, this is it, Alec.

ALEC. Larry?

LARRY. I've still to do Freddie and the other guy. Don't worry, I'll do them properly. But I'm just telling you now, Alec. After this, that's it for me. No more. Let someone else undo all my hard work. I'm done. Finished.

ALEC. Larry, you can't be replaced.

LARRY. Yes I can. If my wife can do it, so can you.

ALEC. And what are you going to do?

NORMAN. I could have a go at it.

LARRY. I'm going to retire, maybe go back to driving taxis again.

ALEC. And I suppose you just happen to have a tidy wee nest egg tucked away. Say, about . . .

LARRY. Don't say nothing, Alec.

ALEC. Well . . .

LARRY. You just talk to them out there. Talk on TV. Talk in big debates. Preach your new brand of Unionism anywhere you want, but these ears are closed to you. And you better do some serious thinking too. Like think about this. Maybe the reason I can't unconvince these young lads about the struggle is because I was so fucking right the first time. Think about that.

LARRY *walks to the door.*

JACK. Where are you going?

LARRY. I'm going to get a bit of air. It stinks in here.

LARRY *leaves.*

JACK. That didn't go very well.

ALEC. I'm sure you must have a lot on your plate, Jack. So, I'll leave you to it.

JACK. No problem. Norman, show Alec out.

NORMAN *leads* ALEC *out of the office.* JACK *begins work again.*

Scene Eight

Living room. Day.

FREDDIE *is now hanging the all white top half of the wallpaper.* KYLE *and* LARRY *enter the room.* FREDDIE *stops working and stands, quickly.*

KYLE. Where's Sandra?

FREDDIE. She took wee Joe up to her Ma's, the paint was doing his head in again, why?

KYLE. Just wondering.

LARRY. Nice work Freddie.

FREDDIE. What's he doing here.

KYLE. You said you wanted to talk, I've brought the only man who would listen. So are you going to talk or not?

FREDDIE *weighs up the situation slowly.* LARRY *waits.*

FREDDIE. Before we start anything, I just want to make sure that we understand each other.

LARRY. Where have you been the last couple of days?

FREDDIE. I haven't been anywhere near the fucking club for a start. And I'll not be going anywhere near it in the future either. Tell Jack I said it's a fucking hole.

KYLE. Larry, I've had a chat with him, if you push it he's just going to say that he didn't do it. So, it'll be his word against Jack's.

FREDDIE. And I wonder who's side you're going to be on.

LARRY. I'm not on anybody's side but my own. We're down thirty-five grand and we want it back.

FREDDIE (*stands*). I can get you it back but I'm not taking the fall for the robbery. My Ma never brought up no thief.

LARRY. There's a few bank managers might challenge that.

FREDDIE. The only bank I ever robbed was Allied Irish.

LARRY. Say I agree to accept that you didn't do it. And say I tell everyone else to accept it – the problem is that that would mean that somebody else robbed us. And somebody else will have to pay for it.

FREDDIE. Stop talking shit, all right.

LARRY. I don't like you, Freddie.

FREDDIE. Same difference.

LARRY. But this isn't about liking or not liking. This is bigger than that.

FREDDIE. Can we stick to points, I don't want any of your daft wee stories.

LARRY. You've got options. But there's a lot of ifs and buts involved.

FREDDIE. Always is.

KYLE. Just listen to him, Freddie.

LARRY. I'm willing to give you the benefit of the doubt. But you're putting the responsibility on your friend's shoulders. If Kyle's willing to vouch for you, that's up to him.

KYLE. I am.

LARRY. Right. Then here it is.

FREDDIE. At last.

LARRY. We have a situation on our hands. We can't have renegades destroying everything that we've achieved.

FREDDIE. You've achieved nothing.

LARRY. I'm not going to debate with you.

FREDDIE. Good.

LARRY (*pauses to consider*). What if I said that the slate's clean, Freddie? We're starting fresh. You and me too. You see we're going to be concentrating more on putting our own house in order for the next few months.

KYLE. It's not a punishment squad – it's different from that.

LARRY. You just give us the money back – name two people that we are going to . . . have to deal with anyway and you can come back on board and help Kyle put a stop to all this nonsense of renegades and breakaway groups.

FREDDIE. I'm not fucking naming anybody.

LARRY. Or what about this, Freddie? (*Pause.*) Say I said that I don't even need to know how or where you get the money back from, maybe you just find it sitting somewhere and you hand it over to us. We get our money back and you get back into your team and everything returns to normality. How does that sound?

FREDDIE. No.

LARRY. What do you mean, no?

FREDDIE. I want guns.

LARRY. You can't have guns.

FREDDIE. Well then you can't have your money back.

KYLE. Freddie, the man's trying to talk to you. You fucked up.
(*Quickly.*) Somebody fucked up. We need to get this sorted
out before things go fucking bananas on us.

FREDDIE. You're doing it again, Kyle.

KYLE. What?

FREDDIE. Backing other people up instead of your best mate.

LARRY. And what are you doing for your best mate?

FREDDIE. Don't talk about things you don't understand,
Larry.

LARRY. What do I not understand?

FREDDIE. You don't understand mates, you don't understand
loyalty.

LARRY. Kyle, talk to him.

FREDDIE. You think I don't know what you've been doing.

KYLE. Freddie?

LARRY. We're wasting time here.

FREDDIE. I've been telling you that for ages. So, why don't
you just stop wasting time and give me the fucking guns
and let me get on with it?

LARRY. I can't do that, Freddie.

KYLE. There's things going on we don't understand. Things
are changing but Larry's on our side. These things are
nothing to do with him or us. These things are out of our
hands. These things are . . . politics.

FREDDIE. Fuck politics, fuck talking, fuck all that shit. Let
me explain something to you here. Taigs hate us and we
hate them. That's the way it is and that's the way it's going
to stay. They were fighting like fuck for ages because we
were on top. Now we have to do the same.

LARRY. We're still on top.

FREDDIE (*laughs*). What fucking world do you live in? Here's
my final offer to you, Larry. Assemble all the good men, get
all the weapons you can and join me. We need a war, and
we need it now. While we've still got a chance of winning it.

LARRY. The war's over Freddie.

FREDDIE. No it's not. Everything's going to blow up, Larry.
Only thing is, if we wait on the taigs doing it, we won't be
ready. The troops'll be gone, the police'll be relaxed and
you and all the other stupid cunts will be too busy sorting
out your own back yards to do fuck all about it. I say we go
now.

LARRY. Then you're going to die, Freddie.

FREDDIE. It's better to die on your feet, than to live on your
knees.

LARRY. And is it better to die on your face. Shot in the back
of the head by your best friend.

FREDDIE. Fuck you.

KYLE. Let's talk properly men.

FREDDIE. I've told you before. Fuck talk.

KYLE. This is your only chance, Freddie. You're talking shite.

FREDDIE. Fuck off, Kyle. You're a dickhead.

LARRY. Listen to your friends, Freddie.

FREDDIE. I'll see who my friends are, when I make my
move.

FREDDIE *moves towards the door.*

KYLE. Wait, Freddie.

FREDDIE. I've been waiting. Waiting on Paisley. Waiting on
Robinson taking over. Waiting on the call. Waiting on
people like Larry here. Well I'm all waited out. It's time.

LARRY. You go out that door, Freddie, you're really fucking
yourself.

FREDDIE. I'm so scared, Larry.

KYLE. Freddie, sit down.

FREDDIE *hands the pasting brush to* KYLE.

FREDDIE. I'm out of here.

KYLE. Look, this is going bad. Why don't we go to the club
and just sit down and thrash it out over a few pints?

LARRY. I'll go.

KYLE. What do you say, Freddie?

LARRY. Your best mate's reaching his hand out. That's the hand of salvation.

FREDDIE. See he's only going to talk shit like that, Kyle. There's no point.

KYLE. For fuck sake, Freddie. I've done everything I can for you. What about doing something for me?

FREDDIE. I'm going to do something for you. I'm going to fight the people who are trying to take over your country. Now you have a choice to make. You can come with me and we'll fight the scum together or you can stay here with bullshitters like him.

LARRY. Go on out. Tired listening to you.

KYLE. What can I say? What do you want me to do – beg?

FREDDIE. I want you to do what you're supposed to do. Be a man. Don't be his wee boy.

KYLE. Come on, Freddie.

FREDDIE. Look at him. Him and his mates were our heroes, Kyle. They were going to protect us. Look at him – I can't believe I used to look up to such a small man.

LARRY. Let him go, Kyle.

KYLE. This is the last time I'm going to ask you.

FREDDIE. Thank fuck for that. I'm getting tired of listening to your whinging.

KYLE. Fuck you.

FREDDIE *leaves, laughing.*

LARRY. That's it.

KYLE. Give me a few minutes. I'll go and talk to him again.

LARRY. No time, Kyle.

KYLE. I'll sort it.

LARRY. You wanted me to come and listen to him and I've done that for you, Kyle. Haven't I?

KYLE. You have.

LARRY. I know he's your mate and it's a hard thing to do but don't let him fuck everything up.

KYLE. What am I supposed to do?

LARRY. Like he says – be a man. Get the rest of your team. Get me my money back and put him out of circulation. Today.

KYLE *thinks.*

KYLE. I don't want my team doing this.

LARRY. It has to be done, Kyle.

KYLE. Then we'll have to do it ourselves. Me and you.

LARRY. It's your call.

Scene Nine

Punishment room. Evening.

FREDDIE *is tied to a chair.* KYLE *is standing behind him.* LARRY, JACK *and* NORMAN *are sitting in the chairs a few feet behind* FREDDIE.

KYLE. Who robbed the club, Freddie?

FREDDIE. Suck my dick, Kyle, will you?

KYLE *punches* FREDDIE *in the lower back.* FREDDIE *reacts, angrily.*

KYLE. We know it was you, Freddie. But we need to know who the other guy was.

FREDDIE. Get these fucking things off me! You fucking faggot bastard!

KYLE *punches him on the opposite side of his lower back.*

KYLE. Who helped you rob the club, Freddie?

FREDDIE. Fuck you!

NORMAN. Let me talk to him. (NORMAN *swings a cricket bat through the air.*)

KYLE. Relax, Norman.

LARRY. This is only the beginning, Freddie. After we make you confess we have other questions that need to be answered. (*Pause.*) Talk to Kyle, Freddie. He's your friend.

FREDDIE. He's a traitor bastard. Aren't you, Kyle? You half-baked taig loving whore. (KYLE *slaps* FREDDIE *in the face.* FREDDIE *struggles, desperately, to free himself.*) You fucking yellow cunt. Let me out of this.

KYLE. Answer the question.

KYLE *hits* FREDDIE *again, this time it hurts and* FREDDIE *needs time to recover.*

JACK. Larry, I really don't want to be here. This isn't my scene, you know me. Couldn't I just head on and leave . . .

KYLE. You're a witness Jack. You have to be here.

JACK. But I've done all I can do, what's the point in me just standing here.

LARRY. Kyle's running the show, not me, Jack. Ask him.

NORMAN. I don't like just standing here either. Can't I question him a wee bit?

KYLE. Shut up, Norman! (*To* JACK.) What's the problem Jack?

JACK. I'm just saying I don't want to be here, that's all. I mean, I've told you all I can tell you.

KYLE. But Freddie might tell us who the other guy was and then I would need to check that with you.

JACK. Larry?

LARRY. That's true, Jack. But if you don't want to watch, stand outside until you're needed.

JACK. OK.

JACK *attempts to leave.* KYLE *blocks his path.*

KYLE. You're going nowhere.

LARRY. Kyle, let him go. He doesn't have the stomach for this, he never did.

KYLE. That man there. Look at him. Look at him! (JACK *does.*) That man's my best friend and he's strapped to that chair because of your testimony. So you sit down and you wait and see what happens to people who tell me lies.

JACK. I've always told you the truth.

KYLE. Well then you've nothing to worry about.

KYLE *realises that* FREDDIE *has recovered so he grabs* JACK *and drags him to* FREDDIE.

JACK. What are you doing?

KYLE. Freddie, Jack here says that he saw you – he recognised you.

JACK. Larry, this isn't right.

KYLE. What do you have to say about that, Freddie?

FREDDIE. Fuck him and fuck you.

JACK *breaks free and rushes away.*

KYLE. People make mistakes, Freddie. Robbing our club is not the way we do business. Somebody fucked up and somebody has to pay. Jack says it's you. But it's not that simple, because it wasn't just you, Freddie. Two fuck-ups fucked up and we need both of them.

JACK. So, now that we all know that it was him, I'm not needed. Isn't that right, Larry?

KYLE. Just sit down, Jack.

LARRY *nods at* JACK *and then at a chair.* JACK *sits down.*

KYLE. There's two ways we can do this, Freddie. We can keep on hurting you until you break, and you know you will break sooner or later but why when there's another way. Tell me who the other guy is and we'll bring them in and make them tell us where the money is. What do you say? (*Pause.*) Maybe it was all their idea. Maybe this mad fuckhead plan was nothing to do with you, Freddie. Maybe you're the innocent pawn here. Am I right?

FREDDIE. Fuck this! Come on, get it over with. Kill me – don't make me listen to this shit.

FREDDIE *begins to laugh.*

KYLE. Would you rather Norman talked to you?

NORMAN. I would get somewhere. This isn't working, Larry.

KYLE. Help me, Freddie. And I'll help you.

FREDDIE. OK. OK.

LARRY. Back off Norman.

FREDDIE. Untie me and I'll tell you.

JACK. No way. No way, you can't untie him.

NORMAN. We can't do that, Larry.

FREDDIE. Untie me, Kyle.

KYLE *looks at* LARRY. LARRY *indicates that it is* KYLE's *decision.*

KYLE. Tell me first.

FREDDIE. Come on. There's four of you. Take these off. I'm not going to do anything. Look at me, I'm fucked.

KYLE. Tell me first.

FREDDIE. There was no-one else.

JACK. There was two of you. I seen you's.

FREDDIE. Look, it's his word against mine, maybe he thought he seen two of us because of the blow to the head that I gave him.

LARRY. Are you admitting this now?

FREDDIE. I am, but only if we all agree it was just me. I was going to buy some stuff by myself for myself. Because I am a one man fucking army.

KYLE. You don't know how to buy stuff, Freddie.

NORMAN. Let me talk to him.

LARRY *nods.* NORMAN *walks forward.* KYLE *steps between them.* NORMAN *points the bat into* KYLE's *chest.*

KYLE. I'm sorting this.

NORMAN. You had your chance. Now it's Norman's turn.

KYLE. Larry, I've got him to confess, let me keep going here.

LARRY. You've got five minutes.

NORMAN. Then it's over to me?

FREDDIE. What are you going to do with that Norman?

NORMAN. That's for me to know and you to find out.

KYLE. Don't do this to yourself, Freddie. Talk to me now.

FREDDIE. I just want you to know, Norman. (*Pause.*) You touch me once with that bat, you better make sure you kill me.

JACK. Can I go now that he's admitted everything?

KYLE. What did I tell you?

FREDDIE. I'm going to come back, Norman. And I will fuck you, and I'll fuck your wife, your daughter . . . Have you got a dog Norman?

KYLE. Shut up, Freddie.

FREDDIE. I'm just saying.

KYLE. Well fucking don't bother, all right.

LARRY. Ask him now Kyle? For the last time.

NORMAN. Did you hear what he said? Let me ask him.

KYLE. Last chance Freddie.

FREDDIE. Tell me this Kyle. How long have we been best friends?

KYLE. What do you want to say Freddie?

FREDDIE. I've always treated you like a brother. We've fought together, we've robbed together and we've killed together. Am I right or wrong?

NORMAN. Fuck this!

KYLE. Let him say his piece.

FREDDIE. Thank you.

KYLE. Don't tear the arse out of it.

FREDDIE. When little Joe was born did you not call me Uncle Freddie?

LARRY. Don't listen to him Kyle.

FREDDIE. What are you going to tell him about this? What are you going to tell Sandra?

KYLE. This is where you have it all fucked up, Freddie. This isn't happening to you because of me. This is happening to me because of you.

Silence.

FREDDIE. Oh really. Well, from where I'm sitting it looks like . . . (*Stops, hurting.*)

KYLE. What?

FREDDIE. Doesn't matter.

NORMAN. Are we just going to stand here all day or what?

FREDDIE. Why don't you cross yourself with that bat and give me ten Hail Mary's?

KYLE. Fuck up, Norman! (*To* FREDDIE.) Freddie, this is it! This really is it. No more fucking around. Time is up. You robbed the club – you want to buy guns to start your own private fucking war and it's all over now. It's all fucked.

FREDDIE *begins to whistle the tune to the 'Billy Boys'.*

Are you listening to me? Out there is at least one more crazy bastard with a shitload of money, who could put everything in jeopardy for us and our kids. Give me the name of that bastard or so help me I will fucking split you open.

FREDDIE. Here's the deal.

NORMAN. No time for deals.

KYLE. Fuck up. (*To* FREDDIE.) Make it quick.

FREDDIE. I'll get you the money back but I can't tell you who the other person is.

KYLE. What do you say, Larry?

LARRY. Where's the money?

FREDDIE. That's my problem. They have it.

KYLE. Who?

FREDDIE. My mate.

KYLE. Was it Dougie or Mac?

FREDDIE. I said I'm not telling you.

LARRY. Where's the money, Freddie.

NORMAN. This is all shite.

FREDDIE. Let me go and I swear to God I'll get you your money and I'll come straight back here with it.

JACK. No way. You can't let him leave here.

NORMAN. Jack's right. This is all a trick to get him out of here.

JACK. Once he's free, Larry. He'll come after us.

NORMAN. We'll never get another chance like this.

KYLE. Fuck you.

FREDDIE. Help me out here, Kyle. This is the way it has to be.

NORMAN. Bullshit, let me beat it out of him.

KYLE. Hold it! (*To* FREDDIE.) Tell me, Freddie. Just whisper a name and a place and I'll go get it. I promise I will never tell another living soul.

FREDDIE. I can't Kyle.

KYLE. You have to mate.

FREDDIE. Please. Let me go.

NORMAN. Is that five minutes yet, Larry?

LARRY. It's not working Kyle. Norman!

> NORMAN *closes in.* KYLE *tries to stop him.* NORMAN *swings the bat at* KYLE. *Misses and attempts to get him with it in the opposite direction.* KYLE *punches him before he can make it happen.* NORMAN *drops the bat and* KYLE *picks it up.*

KYLE. Fuck it! The next person that moves gets this for lunch. Is that clear? Is that crystal fucking clear?

Everyone stops, still.

LARRY. Kyle. Kyle this is going wrong, mate.

JACK. Thick as thieves. That's what this looks like.

FREDDIE. That's it. And that's only the start of it, Norman. Once I get out of here I'm going to fuck you like you never been fucked before.

KYLE. Shut up, Freddie. I mean it.

FREDDIE. Untie me, mate. Two against three.

JACK. Two against two, I'm not against anybody.

LARRY. Shut up, Jack.

FREDDIE (*laughing*). What a yellow bastard you are, Jack?

KYLE. Fuck up, Freddie. Don't you get it? Don't you see? It's not three against two mate. It's thousands against you.

FREDDIE. I like them odds.

KYLE. Will you listen to me? You're fucked here. I need you to tell me who has the money. The only way out of this is to get them to hand the money back, Freddie. That's the only thing that's going to make this go away.

JACK. He has to take back everything that he said too. All the threats.

KYLE. So, it's all down to you, mate. What's it going to be?

FREDDIE. I see a picture, Kyle. A picture of you in a United Ireland.

KYLE. Just give me a place or a name.

FREDDIE. Do you know what you're doing?

KYLE. No bullshit – just tell me where the money is.

FREDDIE. You're standing watching little Joe getting fucked by a priest.

KYLE *walks away and hands the bat to* NORMAN. NORMAN *begins to beat* FREDDIE *with it.* LARRY *bows his head.* FREDDIE *is eventually covered in blood, battered and bruised. His chair has fallen over on its side. When* KYLE *stops it* FREDDIE *is still tied to the chair.* KYLE *leans beside him, checking his breathing.* LARRY *and* NORMAN *are hovering on either side.* JACK *walks to the door.*

LARRY. Give him a minute to come round and then start again.

JACK. I think we should kill him. After he tells us, we have to do him.

KYLE. Don't be stupid. I'm taking him to the hospital.

JACK. What do you say, Larry?

NORMAN. Jack's got a point.

KYLE. Nobody's killing nobody. That wasn't the deal, Larry. I have to get him to the hospital.

LARRY. I can't let you do that, Kyle. He has to tell us where the money is.

KYLE. He'll tell me in the hospital and I'll get it for you, Larry. (*Pause.*) Trust me, once we're away from here it'll be different. I should have just talked to him on my own in the first place. Honestly Larry, I'll get your money back.

LARRY *thinks.*

LARRY. You're putting me in a serious fucking corner here, Kyle.

KYLE. I've always come through for you, Larry.

JACK. It's you I'm thinking of, Norman. He's going to come after you first.

KYLE. Fuck up, Jack.

NORMAN. You were the witness against him.

JACK. But I never touched him. And he didn't threaten my daughter.

NORMAN *rushes forward and batters* FREDDIE *again.*

KYLE. Get away from him.

KYLE *grabs the bat off* NORMAN. JACK *and* NORMAN *step back.* LARRY *rushes to check* FREDDIE*'s pulse.*

JACK. Don't be stupid, Kyle.

LARRY. Fuck me!

NORMAN. We have to finish it.

JACK. This man is a danger to our families.

LARRY (*to* NORMAN). You are a fuck up.

NORMAN. What do you mean?

LARRY. We're not going to get fuck all out of him for a long time.

NORMAN. What are we going to do?

LARRY. Do whatever the fuck you's like but let me tell you this, Norman, if he doesn't come round or if he does but he can't remember or any shit like that, then you better find 35 grand very fucking fast. Do you hear me?

LARRY *walks away.*

JACK. Where are you going?

LARRY. I'm going home.

JACK. You can't do that.

LARRY. Watch me.

LARRY *leaves.* NORMAN *and* JACK*'s attention returns to* KYLE.

JACK. You always said you could do him, Norman. Now's your chance.

KYLE. I don't give a fuck about, Norman, Jack. I just want you to know that if anybody moves, I'll bash your head to fuck. He can do me afterwards if he wants.

JACK. Wait!

NORMAN. It's your call, Jack.

JACK. Do you think you can take him first, Norman?

NORMAN. Maybe.

NORMAN *steps towards* KYLE. KYLE *raises the bat in preparation to hurt* JACK. JACK *stops* NORMAN.

JACK. He looks dead already, any way.

After JACK *and* NORMAN *leave,* KYLE *throws the bat at the door. Then sits with* FREDDIE. *After checking his pulse again, he slowly and awkwardly picks* FREDDIE's *body up. He struggles but manages to carry him out.*

Scene Ten

Living room. Night.

SANDRA *gets up as* KYLE *enters the living room.*

SANDRA. Oh it's you.

KYLE. That's lovely.

SANDRA. Well what do you expect?

KYLE. Where's Joe?

SANDRA. He's in my Ma's.

KYLE. He's always in your Ma's. He'll be thinking he lives there.

SANDRA. He's staying in my Ma's until we get this place finished.

KYLE (*looks around the room*). What's not finished about it?

SANDRA. It's just not finished, all right?

KYLE. Whatever you say.

SANDRA. It's not finished because Freddie wants to do a good job for us. And anyway I don't see you doing very much about it.

KYLE. I helped him scrape it, didn't I?

SANDRA. If it had've been left to you, you would've just put a wee drop of paint on it and left it like that. So, if you've nothing fucking good to say about it, say nothing.

KYLE. All right, all right. Give me a break from all that – I'm shattered.

SANDRA. I don't give a fuck.

KYLE. Wise up.

SANDRA. I have wised up, when are you going to wise up?

KYLE. Sandra. Stop for two seconds.

SANDRA. What?

KYLE. Look. (*Pause.*) Why don't you go and get wee Joe. I'll get us a chinese and some beers, we'll eat and drink and then we'll have an early night with the three of us curled up in bed watching the tele, just like the old days. What do you say?

SANDRA (*looks around herself*). Are you talking to me?

KYLE. Or what about I go out and come back in and start this again?

SANDRA. What about you go out and find the old Kyle and tell him he can come back and start this again.

KYLE. I am the old Kyle.

SANDRA. I don't know who you are.

KYLE. What are you talking about?

SANDRA. You! I don't know you.

KYLE. Don't be stupid.

SANDRA (*hesitates*). The old Kyle never thought I was stupid.

KYLE. Sorry.

SANDRA. You're not him, you're a stranger.

KYLE. I'm me.

SANDRA. I'm going to go. Fuck you.

KYLE. Is that your answer to everything?

SANDRA. What if it is?

KYLE (*shouts*). Fuck!

SANDRA. Fuck what?

KYLE. Fuck nothing. Sandra, listen to me.

SANDRA. No, you listen to me for once in your life.

KYLE. OK. Go. (*Waits.*) I'm listening to you.

SANDRA (*thinks for a while*). No.

KYLE. What?

SANDRA. I've nothing to say to you. (*Walks towards door.*) If Freddie calls round tell him he doesn't have to do any more 'cause it's finished.

KYLE. Sandra, wait. I have to talk to you.

SANDRA. Tired listening to your shite.

KYLE. This isn't going right.

SANDRA. You're telling me?

KYLE. We have to talk.

SANDRA. Fuck talk.

KYLE. It's about Freddie.

SANDRA. What about him?

KYLE. He's not coming round.

SANDRA. He said he was.

KYLE. Well I'm saying he's not.

SANDRA. Why are you going to stop him?

KYLE. We had to talk to Freddie today.

SANDRA. What do you mean?

KYLE. He went too far.

SANDRA. Hold on, who's we?

KYLE. Have you seen him hanging around with anybody new?

SANDRA. Who's 'we' I asked you.

KYLE. This is important Sandra, Who's new on the scene with Freddie?

SANDRA. Nobody. Now answer my question.

KYLE. Has anybody been here helping him?

SANDRA. Only me.

KYLE. Who were you's drinking with the other night?

SANDRA. What is this?

KYLE. I need to know, Sandra.

SANDRA. What for?

KYLE. Because I have to speak to them.

SANDRA. There was nobody drinking with us, Kyle. There is nobody new on the scene, Kyle. What part of nobody do you not understand?

KYLE (hesitates). Fuck me!

SANDRA. What?

KYLE. Where were you yesterday?

SANDRA. Fuck you, Kyle. Where is Freddie?

KYLE. You were with him, weren't you?

SANDRA. Here's how it works – you answer one of my questions then I answer one of yours. Now get it right for fuck's sake.

KYLE. No time for games Sandra. Did you and Freddie do the club?

SANDRA. You haven't answered one of my questions yet.

KYLE. Freddie's in the hospital.

SANDRA. What?

KYLE. Your turn.

SANDRA. What hospital?

KYLE. Your turn.

SANDRA. See if you're saying what I think you're saying.

KYLE. This is fucking serious, Sandra.

SANDRA. Oh, you finally worked that out did you?

KYLE. Look me in the eye and tell me you weren't with him when he robbed the club.

SANDRA. Go and fuck yourself.

KYLE. Where's the money, Sandra?

SANDRA. What money?

KYLE. Don't fuck around here. Have you got it or has he got it?

SANDRA. I'm not telling you.

KYLE. I need that fucking money, Sandra.

SANDRA. What are you going to do, take me to one of your wee punishment rooms and beat the shite out of me until I tell you everything you want to know? Is that what you're going to do or is that just something you keep for your best friends?

KYLE *grabs* SANDRA *and forces her against the wall.*

KYLE. Have you any idea what you've done? I mean did you ever stop to think for one single fucking second about what you were doing? What you were doing to me – us – Joe?

SANDRA *spits in* KYLE's *face.* KYLE *hesitates before he lets her go.* SANDRA *walks very slowly out of the house.* KYLE *follows her out of the living room but returns carrying a tin of beer.* KYLE *takes a sheet off one of the chairs and sits. He takes a drink of beer and searches for the phone. He finds a wire and eventually it leads him to the phone that is tucked in under the sheet at the side of the other chair. He picks up the receiver and dials a number, then suddenly as it rings begins to batter the phone with it until he lifts it and throws it at the wall. He remains sitting. He takes another drink of beer. He thinks for a while and then begins to laugh.* KYLE *laughs louder and louder.*

The End.